PREFACE

This book will help students determine a sentence's main point by giving them the tools they need to recognize the subject, verb, and modifiers. Designed for entering college students, this book is suitable for courses in basic reading and writing, particularly those that include work in a learning laboratory or tutorial center.

Features include:

- Structural rather than grammatical approach. Word groups such as infinitive phrases, participial phrases, and clause modifiers, while identified as such, are all defined as meaning units. The subject of a sentence is defined as the first noun or pronoun that is not part of a meaning unit.

- Abundant examples of each sentence pattern. These allow students to observe how words work together and to arrive at useful generalizations of their own.

- Practical explanation of basic terminology. Terms such as noun, verb, adjective, adverb, phrase, and clause are defined then illustrated in a variety of contexts. The goal is sentence comprehension.

- Self-correcting exercises that allow students to check their understanding after each lesson.

- Checkpoint exercises that encourage students to interact with instructors, instructional assistants, or tutors.

- Review of key points at the end of each chapter.

- Comprehensive practice exercises at the end of the book. These pinpoint areas needing further study.

- Friendly, supportive style.

By mastering this self-paced book, students can better comprehend the variety of sentences they will encounter in their college reading, especially those sentences in which the subject is conceptual rather than concrete.

ACKNOWLEDGMENTS

I am indebted to the Chabot-Las Positas Community College District for their support with earlier versions of this book, as well as to my colleagues for their suggestions and support. These include Cindy Ahre, Janice Albert, and Jane Benham. I am particularly grateful to Peggy Riley for helping me edit the manuscript.

For the basic approach and organization, I am indebted to Ellen Owens, former instructor at Las Positas College and one of my primary mentors. For the core concepts, I acknowledge Frank Smith, author of *Understanding Reading: A Psycholingusitic Analysis of Reading and Learning to Read,* 3rd Ed. New York: Holt, Rinehart, and Winston, 1982.

INTRODUCTION

The Two Parts of a Sentence

When you speak or write, you are usually creating sentences—groups of words with which you say something about somebody or something.

The thing or person you are talking about is the SUBJECT of the sentence. What you are saying about that person or thing is the VERB.

A couple of simple exercises will show you how much you already know about subjects and verbs.

Insert an appropriate word in each space below. Your word will be a **subject**.

1. The _____ will start at 8:00 p.m.

2. Some _____ spoiled in the refrigerator.

3. A crazy _____ showed up last night.

4. _____ can be fun.

Whatever you put in each blank is the thing or person about which you are saying something. If you put "movie" or "concert" in the blank for number one, then the "movie" or the "concert" is the subject. If you put "surfing" or "cooking" in the blank for number four, then "surfing" or "cooking" is the subject.

Insert an appropriate word in each space below. Your word will be a **verb**.

1. The doctor _____ at her patient.

2. My parakeet _____ better than yours.

3. Italy _____ my favorite country.

4. Ron _____ with the dean.

You may have written something like "looked" or "yelled" for number one. And you probably used "is" for number three. In any case, you likely didn't have much difficulty finding subjects or verbs for these simple sentences.

What makes some sentences more complicated is the number of words that accompany the subject and verb. These accompanying words are called modifiers.

For example, look at this sentence:

The usually soft-spoken doctor suddenly screamed at her patient.

"Doctor" is the subject and "screamed" is the verb. Every other word in the sentence describes either the subject or the verb.

Those words which give a more specific idea of "doctor" modify the subject. Those which give a more specific idea of "screamed" modify the verb. The doctor is "usually soft-spoken." These extra words modify the subject.

The doctor "suddenly" screamed "at her patient." "Suddenly" and "at her patient" show when and how the doctor screamed. These extra words modify the verb "screamed."

This sentence, like other sentences, breaks into two parts: 1) the subject and its modifiers, called the **subject cluster**, and 2) the verb and its modifiers, called the **verb cluster**. The subject is underlined once and the verb twice.

Subject Cluster **Verb Cluster**
The usually soft spoken <u>doctor</u> suddenly <u>screamed</u> at her patient.

The purpose of this book is to help you recognize these word groups and to identify the subject and verb. This ability will help you read with greater speed and understanding.

We will talk more about clusters later. For now, you should simply look for the subject and verb.

 **Exercise**

In these sentences, underline the subject once and the verb twice.

Example: Our new <u>teacher</u> <u>speaks</u> five languages.

1. The next door neighbors dance late at night.

2. Our computer store manager is improving the business.

3. At sunrise, 10,000 Yosemite campers ran for the showers.

4. Ben's old Buick, far too big for the garage, had faded from years in the hot sun.

5. Denims purchased at Frank's Big and Tall will shrink after the first washing.

6. Chad sold the Porsche to his now prosperous ex-wife.

7. Bernie's once famous restaurant had become nothing more than a hash house with a fancy menu.

8. The veal baked in heavy cream is my favorite dish.

9. Bernie's house special is shark steak with jellied Moray eel.

10. *For Whom the Bell Tolls* is a novel set during the Spanish Civil War.

Check your answers with the key at the end of the book.

If you had trouble with any of these exercises, don't worry. This book will help you better understand the way sentences work.

I RECOGNIZING NOUNS AND PRONOUNS

How to Identify a Noun

Nouns have three characteristics:

- NOUNS NAME.

    People: Dottie, Mr. Perez
    Places: Australia, Detroit
    Objects: computers, clocks, cuckoos
    Feelings: sadness, excitement
    Ideas: capitalism, practicality
    Actions: working, surfing

- NOUNS ARE OFTEN SIGNALED BY **DETERMINERS**.

    Determiners are **a, an,** and **the.**

        a computer
        an apple
        the city

                                    NOUN
    Be careful when biting into **an** apple.

        NOUN
    The city can be exciting.

Sometimes one or more modifiers come between the determiner and the noun it signals.

        NOUN   NOUN
    A small computer can be **an** inexpensive, entertaining toy.

But nouns do not always take determiners.

        NOUN   NOUN
    Good acting requires hard work.

1

NOUN
Fear can be paralyzing.

- NOUNS MAY BE SINGULAR OR PLURAL.

Singular means one. Plural means more than one and is normally formed by adding **-s** or **-es**.

> computers
> two apples
> a thousand cities

Exercise 1

By looking for one or more of these characteristics of nouns, underline each word that works as a noun in these sentences.

1. The heart is an organ which is difficult to replace.

2. Forests are vital to our environment.

3. The computer has become a necessity in most offices.

4. Dennis knows the cure for your difficulties.

5. Chicago is famous for its architecture.

6. The work is too dangerous.

7. Seattle offers great views.

8. A great view can cost money.

9. Anxiety is a general uneasiness.

10. The view from our cheap room was a disappointment.

Check your answers with the key at the end of the book.

How to Identify a Pronoun

A pronoun is a word that takes the place of a noun.

> Ben loves ice cream. In fact, *he* is a share holder in one of the country's biggest ice cream manufacturers. ("He" takes the place of "Ben.")

But ice cream has a downside. *It* tends to increase the width of its fans. ("It" takes the place of "ice cream.")

These are the personal pronouns:

Singular		**Plural**	
Subject	Object	Subject	Object
I	me	we	us
you	you	you	you
he	him	they	them
she	her		
it	it		

But there are other pronouns as well:

Somebody screamed.
Anybody can come to the party.
This will never do.
Joe wants **something.**
That makes me mad.
Many did not even answer the phone.
One of the doughnuts is poisonous.

Usually pronouns fit in the same slots as nouns:

Joe gave **flowers** to **Maria.**
(**He** gave **them** to **her.**)

The **flowers** were too big for the **vase.**
(**They** were too big for **it.**)

 # Exercise 2

Underline all of the pronouns in each of the following sentences.

1. They walked in quietly, hoping the teacher wouldn't see them.

2. Something was bothering him.

3. Anyone is welcome to come to the concert.

4. Somebody had called the police.

5. During the night, we heard them shouting.

Check your answers with the key at the end of the book.

■■■ How to Determine the
■■ Subject of a Sentence
■

The subject of a sentence is usually the first noun or pronoun. If you can identify the first noun or pronoun of a sentence you are well underway to making good sense of that sentence.

■ The first noun is underlined in these sentences.

> <u>Birds</u> have provided human beings with various forms of entertainment.

> Certain <u>birds</u> have learned to speak.

> Some <u>parrots</u> may understand the rudiments of language.

> <u>Researchers</u> disagree about this claim.

In each of these sentences, the first noun is the subject.

■ The first pronoun is underlined in these sentences.

> <u>They</u> distrust the work of Dr. Featherston, a scientist who believes birds can do no wrong.

> <u>He</u> published a series of articles praising the intelligence of a cockatoo named Cyril.

> However, <u>many</u> question Featherston's research method.

> <u>It</u> involved living with the cockatoo in Featherston's tiny studio apartment, hardly a suitable environment for controlled scientific experiments.

> <u>Someone</u> even questioned Featherston's sanity.

In each of these sentences the first pronoun is the subject.

■■■
■■ Nouns With More Than One Word
■

■ Names of people, places, and institutions may have more than one word, but they are treated as single nouns:

> **Eric Hoffer** was a longshoreman and philosopher.
> **Las Vegas** is a growing city.
> **Proctor and Gamble** sells soap.
> **Indiana University** is noted for its music department.

These names are called **proper nouns.**

- Titles of books, plays, movies, television shows, stories, and magazine articles are treated the same way. (Note: Major titles—books, plays, movies, television shows—are italicized. Other titles are in quotation marks.)

  The Sound and the Fury is one of Faulkner's most admired novels.
  The Donna Reed Show portrays a mother who can solve all problems.
  "The Catbird Seat," a story by James Thurber, illustrates the unreliability of appearances.
  Gone with the Wind features Clark Gable as Rhett Butler and Vivien Leigh as Scarlett O'Hara.

Review

1. Nouns name.

2. Nouns work with determiners.

3. Nouns can be singular or plural.

4. Pronouns can take the place of nouns.

5. The subject of a sentence is usually the first noun or pronoun.

6. Names of people, places, and institutions may have more than one word, but they are treated as single nouns.

7. Titles of books, movies, stories are also treated as single nouns.

Exercise 3

In the following sentences, <u>underline</u> the first noun or pronoun. When you are finished, check your answers with the key at the end of the book.

1. Connections are quite useful.

2. The blintzes were delicious.

3. *Star Wars* is a movie about good and evil.

4. Something always goes wrong.

5. The peak of Mount Rainier is visible from Seattle.

6. The environment has become increasingly important to us.

7. Robert Stack played the role of Elliot Ness in the television series *The Untouchables.*

8. He was a confident, matter-of-fact agent for the FBI.

9. That was just fine.

10. Anyone with money is welcome to come.

II RECOGNIZING VERBS

The verb of a sentence tells what the subject DOES or what the subject IS. It is made up of a main verb (MV) sometimes preceded by one or more helping verbs (HV).

In these sentences, the verb tells what the subject does:

>   MV
> Some people write bad checks.

>   HV   MV
> I have never written a bad check.

>   HV HV   MV
> Brenda's ex-husband has been writing bad checks for years.

In these sentences, the verb tells what the subject is:

>   MV
> Brenda is an honest woman.

>   HV MV
> Her ex-husband has been a crook all of his life.

Main Verbs

Verbs take five different forms:

1. Base Form   Frequently I (cook, drive).

2. -s Form   Frequently he/she (cooks, drives).

3. Past Tense   Yesterday I (cooked, drove).

4. Present Participle   I am (cooking, driving) at the moment.

5. Past Participle   I have (cooked, driven) for years.

Notice that the past tense and the past participle of "cook" is formed by adding -ed. Verbs that follow this pattern are called **regular**. Verbs that do not follow this pattern, such as "drive," are **irregular**.

These are some regular verbs:

Base Form	Past Tense	Past Participle
play	played	played
practice	practiced	practiced
exercise	exercised	exercised

These are some irregular verbs:

Base Form	Past Tense	Past Participle
fight	fought	fought
dig	dug	dug
sing	sang	sung
win	won	won
drive	drove	driven

The verb "be" is very irregular. Its forms are be, am, is, are, was, were, being, and been.

 # Helping Verbs

Some words in English always work as helping verbs, never as main verbs. These are:

can, will, shall, may, might, must, could, should, would

For example:

    HV MV
Mildred will pay her taxes.

    HV   MV
Harold should pay his taxes.

Some words can work as either helping verbs or main verbs. These are:

have, has, had
do, does, did
be, am, is, are, was, were, being, been (forms of the verb be)

For example:

"Has" can work as a helping verb:

        HV MV
Harold has baked peanut butter cookies.

But it can also work as a main verb:

        MV
Harold has peanut butter cookies in his car.

"Did" can work as a helping verb:

     HV   MV
We did attempt to tell the police.

But it can also work as a main verb:

        MV
As usual, I did the dishes.

"Is" follows the same pattern:

     HV MV
Harold is baking the cookies this year.

OR

     MV
Harold is quite a cook.

Exercise 1

For each of the following sentences, put an HV over each helping verb and an MV over each main verb. When finished, check your answers with the key at the end of the book.

1. Our school principal wore ugly suits.

2. Our school principal has often worn ugly suits.

3. Everyone in our family has a cold.

4. My Uncle Homer was a farmer in downstate Illinois.

5. Uncle Homer was milking the cows at daybreak.

6. We must have danced all night.

7. I was a bus driver in Chicago.

9

8. I was driving an express on the near north side.

9. You might have called me first.

10. Terry has been playing the saxophone since childhood.

Infinitives

All verbs have an infinitive form. It is made with the word "to": to walk, to think, to win, to be.

However this infinitive form will never be the verb of a sentence. Instead it will usually follow the verb:

          MV
Maria wants **to be** President of the United States.

      HV   MV
Tim was trying **to save** money.

Exercise 2

For each of the following sentences, put an HV over each helping verb, an MV over each main verb, and an INF over each infinitive. When finished, check your answers with the key at the back of the book.

1. Dr. Salk wanted to find a polio vaccine.

2. Dr. Sabin was looking for an oral vaccine.

3. Parents tried to comfort their children.

4. The nurses were hoping to avoid a strike.

5. Their union had been working on a contract.

Present Participles Used as Nouns

The present participle (-ing form) of a verb can sometimes be used as a noun, naming an action.

Walking is an excellent form of exercise.

Many people hate **dieting**.

When a present participle is the first noun in a sentence, it will be the subject of that sentence:

Walking is an excellent form of exercise.

Flying makes some people nervous.

Stealing is wrong.

 # Review

1. The verb of a sentence tells what the subject DOES or what the subject IS.

2. The verb of a sentence is made up of a main verb sometimes preceded by one or more helping verbs.

3. Regular verbs form the past tense and the past participle with an -ed. Irregular verbs follow other patterns.

4. Some helping verbs can also function as main verbs.

5. The infinitive form of a verb always begins with "to."

6. An infinitive will never be the sentence verb.

7. The present participle of a verb (-ing form) can sometimes function as a noun. As a result, a present participle can sometimes be the subject of a sentence.

Exercise 3

In the following sentences, underline the subject once and the verb twice. Remember that the verb includes the main verb plus all the helping verbs.

Examples: The <u>glass</u> <u>was broken</u>.

Our <u>plane</u> <u>was</u> an old Boeing 727.

<u>We</u> <u>wanted</u> to win the lottery.

<u>Midge</u> <u>had been buying</u> lottery tickets for years.

<u>We</u> <u>hoped</u> to reach Los Angeles by nightfall.

When finished, check your answers with the key at the end of the book.

1. Jessica was working at Bloomingdale's.

2. She had wanted to be a movie star.

3. Some people are dreamers.

4. They are dreaming of better times in better cities.

5. Reading requires an active mind.

6. An estimated 50,000 bees swarmed into a subway station in Rio de Janeiro.

7. They attacked passengers on platforms and in trains.

8. Apparently a tractor had disturbed the beehive.

9. Insects have been known to change people's lives.

10. Termites have devoured house, home, and an occasional shopping mall.

Exercise 4

In the following sentences, underline the subject once and the verb twice. Remember that the verb includes the main verb plus all the helping verbs. When you are finished, take them to an instructor or an instructional assistant to check your answers.

1. Unseasonably warm weather has convinced bears to come out of hibernation.

2. Australian fires charred almost 300 homes.

3. Jessica Mitford angered the funeral industry with her book, *The American Way of Death.*

4. Santa Fe is famous for its opera.

5. Singing takes talent as well as nerve.

6. We hoped to take first place at the state fair.

7. Our ultimate goal was to become the tomato kings of the Sacramento Valley.

8. *Tomatoes I Have Known and Loved* was a best selling book for ambitious farmers.

9. Once again, learning precedes glory.

Instructor/Assistant Check: _____

III   RECOGNIZING ONE-WORD MODIFIERS

■■■ The Subject Cluster and
■ ■ the Verb Cluster

So far you have learned that the subject of a sentence is usually the first noun or pronoun. In the following sentence, the subject is underlined once, and the verb is underlined twice.

> <u>People</u> <u>work</u>.

This sentence is as basic as you can get. "People" is the first and, in this case, the only noun in the sentence—so it is the subject. "Work" tells what the subject does, so it is the verb. To make the sentence more specific, we can add descriptive words called **modifiers**. Here is a slight revision:

> Most <u>people</u> <u>work</u>.

Now it is clear that the majority of people work. The word "most" modifies "people", telling how many. Here is another revision:

> Most <u>people</u> <u>work</u> daily.

Now it is clear that most people work every day. The word "daily" modifies "work", telling how often.

The subject and its modifiers are called the **subject cluster**. Everything else in a sentence is called the **verb cluster**. Here the subject cluster is bracketed:

> [Most <u>people</u>] <u>work</u> daily.

Other sentences work in the same way, no matter how many modifiers are added:

> [Happy <u>customers</u>] <u>will return</u>.

> [Unhappy <u>customers</u>] <u>will return</u> merchandise promptly.

> [A patient, intelligent <u>manager</u>] <u>can pacify</u> the angriest, meanest customer.

The Two Types of Modifiers: Adjectives and Adverbs

Modifiers basically work in two ways. Some further describe nouns or pronouns, while others further describe verbs.

Those that modify nouns or pronouns are called **adjectives**.

Those that modify verbs are called **adverbs**.

In the following sentences, adjectives are marked with an ADJ, and adverbs are marked with an ADV.

     ADJ   ADJ   ADV
[Unhappy <u>customers</u>] <u>will return</u> faulty merchandise promptly.

The first adjective, "unhappy," modifies the noun "customers," telling what kind of customers. The second adjective, "faulty," modifies the noun "merchandise," telling what kind. The adverb "promptly" modifies the verb "will return," telling when.

Notice that only those adjectives modifying the subject (first noun) belong to the subject cluster. Other modifiers, whether they are adjectives or adverbs, belong to the verb cluster.

     ADJ   ADJ   ADV
[A patient, intelligent <u>manager</u>] <u>can</u> usually <u>pacify</u> the
     ADJ   ADJ
angriest, meanest customer.

In this sentence, the first noun "manager" is the subject, and the adjectives "patient" and "intelligent" indicate what kind of manager. "Can pacify" is the verb, and "usually" is an adverb telling when. "Angriest" and "meanest" are adjectives modifying the noun "customer." Notice that adjectives tend to tell **what kind** or **how many**, while adverbs tend to tell **how**, or **when**, or **why**.

     ADJ   ADV
[An old <u>Chevy</u>] <u>sells</u> easily.

"Old" indicates what kind of Chevy. "Easily" tells how it sells.

     ADJ   ADV
[Some <u>Pontiacs</u>] <u>sell</u> immediately.

"Some" indicates how many Pontiacs. "Immediately" tells when they sell.

Exercise 1

In the following sentences, put an ADJ over each adjective and an ADV over each adverb; underline the subject once and the verb twice; then bracket the subject cluster.

Examples:

   ADJ   ADV
[Most students] must work part-time.

                      ADJ
[Everybody] loves juicy gossip.

1. Nosy neighbors can cause big problems.

2. Disposal trucks sometimes awaken light sleepers.

3. We desperately wanted to complain.

4. The local authorities ignored us.

5. The mayor had been reading environmental reports.

6. Olivier finally left the stage.

7. The Romans wanted to rule the whole world.

8. They built a complex infrastructure.

9. It included vast roadways and aqueducts.

10. Some aqueducts still stand.

When finished, check your answers with the key at the end of the book.

Nouns That Work Like Adjectives

Usually a word such as "garbage" will be used as a noun, as in this sentence:

[Garbage] can be a problem.

Here "garbage" is the first noun and therefore the subject of the sentence.

But the word "garbage" functions differently in this sentence:

[Garbage <u>trucks</u>] <u>can awaken</u> light sleepers.

Now the word "garbage" modifies the noun "trucks," telling what kind of truck can awaken light sleepers. Since it modifies a noun, it now works as an adjective. The first noun, and hence the subject, is "trucks."

The function of a word, then, depends upon how it is used in a sentence. Look at this sentence:

[<u>Trucks</u>] <u>filled</u> the parking lot.

Here the word "trucks" functions as a noun. Since "trucks" is the first noun, it is the subject of the sentence.

But the function of "truck" changes in the next sentence:

[Truck <u>stops</u>] <u>are</u> famous for cheeseburgers and pie.

Now the word "truck" functions as an adjective, telling what kind of "stops." The word "stops" is the first noun and is the subject of the sentence.

In this next sentence, the words "truck" and "stop" both function as adjectives, modifying the word "diners":

[Truck stop <u>diners</u>] <u>use</u> gallons of catsup in a single day.

Since "diners" is the first word that functions as a noun, it becomes the subject of the sentence.

Based on these examples, we can now make a useful generalization: When a noun comes directly before another noun, that first noun will function as an adjective.

    ADJ
[A city <u>boy</u>] <u>does</u> not <u>know</u> much about farming.

"City," a word we normally would think of as a noun, now works like an adjective. The first noun and thus the subject is "boy." Here is another example:

    ADJ
[Game <u>shows</u>] <u>have continued</u> to be popular.

"Game" is another word we would usually consider a noun, but here it functions as an adjective. It occupies a slot that could also be filled with more typical adjectives like "funny" or "competitive."

    ADJ
[Funny <u>shows</u>] <u>have continued</u> to be popular.

    ADJ
[Competitive <u>shows</u>] have continued to be popular.

Possessives

Possessives, whether they are made from nouns or pronouns, also work like adjectives. Possessives are words that tell to whom or what something belongs.

■ Possessive Nouns

[Joe's <u>house</u>] <u>is</u> the biggest in town.
(The house belongs to Joe.)

[Seattle's <u>port</u>] <u>is</u> beautiful.
(The port belongs to Seattle.)

Possessives, such as "Joe's" and "Seattle's," no longer work like nouns. Instead of naming, they modify, telling which or what kind of house or port. The word "Joe's" tells which house is the biggest in town. The word "Seattle's" tells which port is beautiful. Since both words modify nouns, they now function as adjectives. Possessives occupy the same slots and work in the same way as more familiar adjectives.

     ADJ
[The blue <u>house</u>] <u>is</u> the biggest in town.
     ADJ
[The old <u>port</u>] <u>is</u> beautiful.

■ Possessive Pronouns

Personal pronouns have possessive forms:

Singular		Plural	
Personal	Possessive	Personal	Possessive
I	my	we	our
you	your	you	your
he	his	they	their
she	her		
it	its		

Like possessive forms of nouns, possessive pronouns fit into the same slots as adjectives and function like adjectives.

[Joe's <u>house</u>] <u>is</u> the biggest in town.
[**His** <u>house</u>] <u>is</u> the biggest in town.

[Seattle's <u>port</u>] <u>is</u> beautiful.
[**Its** <u>port</u>] <u>is</u> beautiful.

Verbs That Work Like Adjectives

In the last chapter you learned that the participle form of a verb can sometimes function as a noun.

> [Swimming] is an excellent form of exercise.

> [I] enjoy swimming.

In each sentence, the word "swimming" occupies a slot typically held by a noun.

However the participle form of a verb can also function like an adjective. It all depends on the sentence. For instance:

> [Swimming pools] are a luxury.

In this sentence, "swimming" comes directly before the noun "pools," telling what kind. Since it modifies a noun, "swimming" works as an adjective. The first noun and therefore the subject is "pools."

When verbs work as **adjectives**, they take two different forms. The one in "swimming pools" is the **present participial** form. This form always ends in -ing: swimming pool, fishing rod, looking glass. The other form is the **past participle**. This form usually ends in -ed: baked potato, parched throat, starched collar. However, the past participles of irregular verbs take a variety of endings: beaten path, frozen food, burst balloon.

Examples:

In these sentences, a present participle modifies a noun.

> [Samantha] inherited a **rocking** horse.

> [A **looking** glass] is a fancy mirror.

In these sentences, a past participle modifies a noun.

> [I] hate **starched** collars.

> [**Frozen** dinners] have improved in the last few years.

Where They Might Show Up: Some Variations With Adjectives And Adverbs

In the examples throughout this chapter, adjectives have come directly before the nouns they modify and have frequently been part of the subject cluster:

> ADJ ADJ ADJ
> [My big blue <u>Honda</u>] <u>sat</u> in the lot.

However adjectives can sometimes appear directly after the noun they modify.

> ADJ   ADJ   ADJ
> [My <u>Honda</u>, big and blue,] <u>sat</u> in the lot.

Since the adjectives "big" and "blue" still refer to "Honda," which is the subject of the sentence, "big" and "blue" continue to belong to the subject cluster.

Like adjectives, adverbs can also move around, even appearing at the beginning of a sentence.

> ADV
> Suddenly [<u>Mona</u>] <u>appeared</u>.

> ADV
> Cautiously [<u>she</u>] <u>inserted</u> the key.

Since "suddenly" and "cautiously" refer to the verb of each sentence, they belong to the verb cluster. As a result they are not bracketed; they do not belong to the subject cluster. "Suddenly" does not tell what kind of person Mona is. It indicates when she appeared. In a similar way, "cautiously" does not describe Mona; it tells how she inserted the key.

Review

1. The subject and its modifiers are called the **subject cluster.** Everything else in a sentence is called the **verb cluster.**

2. Modifiers that describe nouns or pronouns are called **adjectives.** Those that describe verbs are called **adverbs.**

3. When a noun comes directly before another noun, it will function as an adjective.

4. Possessives, whether they are made from nouns or pronouns, also work like adjectives. Possessives are words that tell to whom or what something belongs.

5. Present participles and past participles can work like adjectives

6. The part of speech (noun, pronoun, adjective, or adverb) of a word is determined by the way it is used in a sentence.

7. Adjectives can sometimes appear after the noun they modify; adverbs can sometimes appear at the beginning of a sentence.

 # Exercise 2

In the following sentences, put an ADJ over each adjective and an ADV over each adverb; underline the subject once and the verb twice; then bracket the subject cluster.

Remember: words we know as nouns, pronouns and verbs can function as adjectives. When they do, label them as adjectives.

Examples:

    ADJ   ADV   ADJ
[An old dog] can often be a good friend.

ADJ ADJ   ADJ   ADJ
[Our old Labrador] was a great hunting dog.

  ADJ   ADJ   ADJ ADJ
[My favorite game show host] is Frank Smiley.

    ADJ   ADJ ADJ   ADJ
[Australia's little Koala bear] has become a popular animal.

1. Our camping trip was a real adventure.

2. We had forgotten to bring the cooler.

3. Car sickness was a family trait.

4. Eventually the car's radiator hose broke.

5. Aunt Pearl told corny jokes.

6. The camp ground was noisy and crowded.

7. Our poor dog, flea-bitten and nervous, whined continuously.

8. Horton's store had sold its last bottle of mosquito repellent.

9. The kids, bored and itchy, fought incessantly.

10. Amazingly we survived our dream vacation.

When finished, check your answers with the key at the end of the book.

Exercise 3

In the following sentences, put an ADJ over each adjective and an ADV over each adverb; underline the subject once and the verb twice; then bracket the subject cluster.

1. Supermarket shopping can be a real challenge.

2. Crowds fill every aisle.

3. Some customers, impatient and preoccupied, bump other carts.

4. Increasingly people are reading every label.

5. Their reading habits create further congestion.

6. The fruit and vegetable section is filled with incorrigible squeezers and sorters.

7. Hogwild Stores hopes to solve the crowding problem.

8. Hogwild's president has hired traffic managers.

9. These aisle police will confront any offenders.

10. Hopefully they will halt excessive bumping, reading, squeezing, and sorting.

Have an instructor or instructional assistant check these exercises.

Instructor/Assistant Check _____

IV RECOGNIZING BASIC SENTENCE PATTERNS

■■■ Four Basic Sentence Patterns
■■
■

The sentences you have worked with in this book follow four basic patterns:

- Subject - Action Verb
- Subject - Action Verb - Object
- Subject - Linking Verb - Predicate Adjective
- Subject - Linking Verb - Predicate Noun.

In this chapter you will learn to recognize these patterns.

■ Pattern #1 Subject-Action Verb

In this pattern, the subject performs an action. This kind of sentence answers the question "Who or what does what?"

Subject	Action Verb
My <u>uncle</u>	<u>called</u>.
The <u>Giants</u>	<u>won</u>.

■ Pattern #2 Subject-Action Verb-Object

This kind of sentence answers the question "Who or what does what to whom or what?"

Subject	Action Verb	Object
My <u>uncle</u>	<u>called</u>	me.
The <u>Giants</u>	<u>won</u>	the game.

■ Pattern #3 Subject-Linking Verb-Predicate Adjective

In this pattern, the subject does not perform an action; instead something is being said about the subject. The verb, called a **linking verb**, links the subject with an adjective. The adjective that follows a linking verb is called a **predicate adjective**.

A predicate adjective (PA) describes the subject:

25

Subject	Linking Verb	Predicate Adjective (PA)
My <u>uncle</u>	<u>is</u>	crazy.
The <u>Giants</u>	<u>are</u>	unstoppable.

■ **Pattern #4 Subject-Linking Verb-Predicate Noun**

This pattern works the same way as pattern #3, except that the linking verb is followed by a noun instead of an adjective. The noun that follows a linking verb is called a **predicate noun**.

A predicate noun (PN) renames the subject.

Subject	Linking Verb	Predicate Noun (PN)
My <u>uncle</u>	<u>is</u>	a character.
The <u>Giants</u>	<u>are</u>	the winners.

Both of the patterns that contain a linking verb answer the question: "Who or what is what?"

Linking Verbs Made From "To Be"

All linking verbs connect the subject to either a predicate noun or a predicate adjective. Unlike other verbs, linking verbs do not express an action.

You might find it helpful to think of a linking verb as working like an "equals" sign.

          PA
My dog is friendly.
My dog = friendly.

          PN
My dog is a friend.
My dog = a friend.

Linking verbs (LV) are commonly forms of the verb "to be." This verb has eight forms: **be, am, is, are, was, were, being, been.** Forms of "to be" work this way:

    LV   PN
[I] <u>am</u> the doctor.

    LV   PN
[She] <u>is</u> the boss

                   LV   PN
[They] are the workers.

                   LV   PN
[Ben] was the director.

                              LV   PA
[The employees] were happy.

Some forms of "to be" require helping verbs (HV):

                   HV   LV   PA
[We] have been crazy.

                        HV LV PA
[The doctor] will be angry.

As you have seen, each form of "to be" is followed by either a predicate noun (doctor, boss, workers, director) or a predicate adjective (happy, crazy, angry).

■■■
■ ■   Exercise 1
■

In the following sentences, write an OBJ over each object, a PA over each predicate adjective, and a PN over each predicate noun. Subjects have already been identified, along with linking verbs (LV), action verbs (AV), and helping verbs (HV).

Examples:

                                              AV   OBJ
[Her two-year old lizard] usually eats vegetables.

              LV   PN
[Lizards] are reptiles

                        LV PA
[Some lizards] are ugly.

           LV
1. [Snakes] are reptiles.

                LV
2. [Some snakes] are famous.

                HV   LV
3. [Pythons] have been notorious.

                          AV
4. [These large snakes] consume sizeable animals.

27

5. [A <u>Python</u>] <u>can swallow</u>^{HV AV} a forty-pound pig.

6. [A 16-foot African rock <u>python</u>] once <u>ate</u>^{AV} a 130-pound impala.

7. Afterwards, [the sated <u>snake</u>] <u>relaxes</u>^{AV}.

8. [The python's feeding <u>habits</u>] <u>can be</u>^{HV LV} irregular.

9. Annually [a <u>python</u>] <u>may eat</u>^{HV AV} only eight meals.

10. Clearly [this <u>snake</u>] <u>is</u>^{LV} no pig.

Check your answers with the key at the end of the book.

■■■ ■ ■ ■ Helping Verbs Made From "To Be"

When a "to be" form is followed by an action verb (AV), it functions as a helping verb.

[<u>She</u>] <u>is running</u>.
$$\text{HV} \quad \text{AV}$$

[<u>They</u>] <u>are working</u>.
$$\text{HV} \quad \text{AV}$$

[<u>We</u>] <u>have been searching</u> for the doctor.
$$\text{HV} \quad \text{HV} \quad \text{AV}$$

In these sentences, the forms of "to be" help show the time of the action verb. They do not link the subject with a predicate adjective or a predicate noun.

A comparison can further illustrate the two different ways "to be" works:

To be as a Linking Verb

LV PA
She **is** smart.

LV   PN
She **was** the doctor.

HV LV   PN
She has **been** the doctor

To be as a Helping Verb

HV HV   AV   OBJ
She had **been** studying medicine.

HV AV   OBJ
She **is** studying medicine.

28

To sum up the difference: When a form of "to be" is followed by a predicate noun or predicate adjective, it works as a linking verb. But when a form of "to be" is followed by an action verb, it works as a helping verb.

Exercise 2

In these sentences, each form of "to be" is highlighted. Identify each form of "to be" as either a linking verb or a helping verb. Write LV if it functions as a linking verb or HV if it functions as a helping verb.

Example:

        LV
Tanya **is** the boss.

        HV
Tanya **is** supervising the entire office.

1. Tim had **been** the boss previously.

2. Unfortunately Tim **was** insensitive.

3. The secretaries **were** always complaining about him.

4. He **was** always forgetting their birthdays.

5. Birthdays **are** important to most people.

6. He had **been** trying to remember them.

7. But he **was** hopeless.

8. He **was** neglecting everyone's special day.

9. Tanya **was** aware of his shortcomings.

10. Soon birthday parties **were** her trademark.

Check your answers with the key at the end of the book.

Other Verbs That Can Link

There are other verbs that can link. These include:

                                LV   PA

seem   [Bertha] seems angry.

                                LV   PA

look   [They] looked happy.

                                    LV   PA

appear   [The witness] appeared honest.

                          LV   PA

feel   [I] feel confident.

                          HV LV   PA

become   [He] is becoming impatient.

It's important to note that some of these verbs can also function as action verbs (AV):

                           AV

                [We] looked for a bottle opener.

We do not look like a bottle opener. We are looking for a bottle opener. In this sentence, "looked" is an action verb, not a linking verb. Here is an other example:

                     AV

      [The Police] appeared at our door.

The police do not appear to be a door. They showed up at the door. Here "appeared" is an action, indicating what the police did.

To determine whether one of these verbs is working as a linking verb or an action verb, check to see if a predicate adjective or a predicate noun follows. If there is a predicate adjective or a predicate noun then the verb links. If there isn't, the verb expresses action.

Exercise 3

In each of these sentences, identify each highlighted word as either an action verb or a linking verb. Write AV above each action verb and LV above each linking verb.

1. Rose **appeared** lost.

2. She **looked** dizzy.

3. We had **looked** for her all morning.

4. Earlier she had **felt** ill.

5. Denna **felt** Rose's pulse.

Check your answers with the key at the end of the book.

Past Participles After a Linking Verb

As you learned in Chapter Two, past participles can function as adjectives.

A **confused** dog will chase its tail.

Here the past participle "confused" describes the noun "dog." But it's also possible for a past participle to follow a linking verb and function as a predicate adjective. For example:

```
          LV   PA
The dog is confused.
```

The word "confused" still describes the dog. Notice that "confused" fits into the same slot as other predicate adjectives such as these:

```
         LV  PA
The dog is dizzy.
```

```
         LV  PA
The dog is crazy.
```

However in sentences that end in an object, the past participle combines with a helping verb and functions as an action verb.

```
                    HV      AV        OBJ
Your instructions have confused the dog.
```

Here are two more examples of a past participle functioning in these two different ways:

Past participle functioning as the verb:

```
      HV    AV         OBJ
We have broken all the dishes.
("Broken" tells what we have done.)
```

Past participle functioning as a predicate adjective:

         LV   PA
All the dishes are **broken**.
("Broken" describes the dishes.)

Also notice that a past participle can follow other types of linking verbs:

         LV   PA
Madeline appeared **confused**.

         LV   PA
The doctor looked **tired**.

Present Participles After a Linking Verb

As you also learned in Chapter Two, present participles can function as adjectives.

A **boring** class can ruin your morning.

Here the present participle "boring" modifies the subject noun "class."

But as with the past participle, the present participle can also function as a predicate adjective:

         LV PA
My biology class was **boring**.

Here "boring" works like an adjective, describing the subject "class." Since it follows a linking verb, it is a predicate adjective.

If an object follows the present participle, then the present participle functions as an action verb. It now tells what the subject is doing:

         HV   AV   OBJ
Professor Snortum was **boring** the class.

Here is another example of a present participle working in these two different ways:

Present participle functioning as the verb:

         HV   AV   OBJ
Philbert's bad manners were **annoying** his sister.
("Annoying" tells what Philbert was doing.)

Present participle functioning as the predicate adjective:

LV   PA

Philbert's bad manners were **annoying**.
("Annoying" describes his manners.)

To further determine whether a present participle is working as an action verb or as a predicate adjective, simply ask whether the present participle tells what the subject is doing or if it describes the subject. If it tells what the subject is doing, the present participle functions as an action verb:

HV AV

Uncle Ernesto is sleeping.
("Sleeping" tells what Uncle Ernesto is doing.)

OR

HV   AV   OBJ

Uncle Ernesto is frightening the children.
("Frightening" also tells what he is doing.)

But if the present participle describes the subject, it is functioning as a predicate adjective:

LV   PA

Uncle Ernesto is frightening.
(Here "frightening" describes the character of Uncle Ernesto; it does not tell what he is doing.)

 # Review

1. There are four basic sentence patterns:

Subject – Action Verb
Subject – Action Verb – Object
Subject – Linking Verb – Predicate Adjective
Subject – Linking Verb – Predicate Noun.

2. A predicate adjective describes the subject; a predicate noun renames the subject.

3. When a form of "to be" is followed by a predicate noun or predicate adjective, it functions as a linking verb. But when a form of "to be" is followed by an action verb, that form of "to be" functions as a helping verb.

4. Certain other verbs can function as linking verbs. These include seem, appear, look, feel, become.

5. A past or present participle can function as a predicate adjective.

Exercise 4

With each of the following sentences, underline the subject once and the verb twice; then bracket the subject cluster.

Label the parts of the verb: HV for helping verb, AV for action verb, and LV for linking verb. Label objects OBJ, predicate adjectives PA, and predicate nouns PN.

Examples:

                    HV   AV   OBJ
    [Aunt Elvira] was changing a tire.

             HV   AV
    [Elwood] was relaxing.

                        LV   PA
    [The guitar music] was relaxing.

                              LV   PA
    [The whippoorwill's song] was beautiful.

             HV LV   PN
    [Granny] had been the boss.

1. The robbery was a failure.

2. The robbers were clumsy.

3. They had forgotten to bring a bag.

4. Bugsy was drunk.

5. Lefty was confused.

6. Cheezy looked tired.

7. Their car battery was dead.

8. The police were watching them.

9. The bank manager had seen Cheezy's picture.

10. The burglar alarm was shrieking.

When you are finished, have an instructor or instructional assistant check your answers.

Instructor/Assistant Check _____

V   RECOGNIZING PHRASE MODIFIERS

Earlier you learned that there are two kinds of modifiers: adjectives and adverbs. Adjectives (ADJ) modify nouns or pronouns and adverbs (ADV) modify verbs.

     ADJ   ADV   ADJ
The old farmer eventually finished his work.

"Old" describes the "farmer," and "his" modifies "work." The adverb "eventually" modifies "finished."

In this chapter you will learn about **phrase modifiers,** groups of words that work like adjectives or adverbs. We define phrase modifiers as **meaning units.** A meaning unit is a group of words that functions like one word.

Prepositional Phrases

One kind of phrase modifier is the prepositional phrase. Prepositional phrases can work as either adjectives or adverbs.

For example:

    The farmer **on the hill** finished his work.

"On the hill" describes the farmer. Since this prepositional phrase modifies a noun, it is working as an adjective.

    The farmer on the hill finished his work **by nightfall.**

"By nightfall" tells when he finished his work. Since this prepositional phrase modifies a verb, it is working as an adverb.

Prepositional phrases always begin with **a preposition,** a small word that states some kind of relationship such as space, time, comparison, or opposition.

There are lots of prepositions. Here are some of them:

about the problem	**above** the table	**aboard** the plane
across the field	**after** the murder	**against** the law
along the shore	**amid** the confusion	**among** the victims
around the block	**at** bat	**beneath** the umbrella
beside the river	**by** the ocean	**despite** her warnings
for the school	**inside** the brain	**near** Vancouver
of Irish ancestry	**on** Wednesday	**over** the rainbow
to the store	**toward** Miami	**until** dawn
under the bed	**up** the ladder	**with** a hammer

Notice that each preposition is followed by a noun. "About" is followed by the noun "problem." "Above" is followed by the noun "table." "Aboard " is followed by the noun "plane."

To summarize:

1. Prepositional phrases always begin with a small word showing some kind of relationship. For example:

Relationship
space: aboard, among, below, behind, inside, near, with,
time: after, before, until, during
comparison: as, like
opposition: except, contrary to

2. Prepositional phrases always end with a noun.

Exercise 1

In the sentences below, identify each prepositional phrase by circling the preposition, then underlining the rest of the prepositional phrase.

Examples:
   Yvette's Aunt Augusta (from) Boston was the terror (of) the family.

   Augusta was arriving (on) the evening flight.

1. At daybreak, Yvette was preparing for Augusta's visit.

2. She dragged the vacuum cleaner up the stairs and into the guest room.

3. She vacuumed above the windows and under the bed.

4. With a toothbrush, she scrubbed between the bathroom tiles.

5. Despite Yvette's backbreaking efforts, Augusta complained about cat hair.

Check your answers with the key at the end of the book.

■ Where Prepositional Phrases Might Appear

Like other modifiers, prepositional phrases tend to be close to the words they modify. As illustrated in the sentences below, prepositional phrases usually come directly **after** the word they describe.

> A dog **with fleas** makes few friends.
> The president **of the company** fired everyone.
> Some musicians **from Guatemala** arrived this morning.

In these sentences, each prepositional phrase follows the noun that it modifies. What kind of dog makes few friends? A dog with fleas. Which president fired everyone? The president of the company. What kind of musicians arrived? Some musicians from Guatemala.

The pattern is similar when a prepositional phrase modifies a verb.

> I will walk **along the river.**
> Bernardo looked **through the telescope.**

In these sentences, each prepositional phrase follows a verb that it modifies. Where will I walk? Along the river. Where did Bernardo look? Through the telescope.

Even when prepositional phrases stack up on each other, each prepositional phrase will still modify the the previous word.

> Augusta was arriving **on the evening flight from Boston.**

"On the evening flight" works as an adverb, telling when she was arriving. "From Boston" works as an adjective, telling which flight.

Or

> Augusta complained **about cat hair behind the dresser.**

"About cat hair" works as an adverb, telling what she complained about. "Behind the dresser" works as an adjective, giving the location of the cat hair.

■ Identifying the Subject Cluster

By recognizing prepositional phrases and knowing what they modify, you will be better able to identify the subject and the subject cluster. Prepositional phrases are highlighted in these sentences:

> A dog **with fleas** makes few friends.
> The president **of the company** fired everyone.
> Some musicians **from Guatemala** arrived this morning.

The subject cluster, defined as the subject and its modifiers, can be identified as follows. The subject is underlined once, and the verb is underlined twice. The subject cluster is bracketed.

[A dog with fleas) makes few friends.
[The president of the company] fired everyone.
[Some musicians from Guatemala] arrived this morning.

Everything outside of the subject cluster belongs to the verb. This principle is particularly important when a prepositional phrase occurs at the very beginning of a sentence.

Aboard the ship, people were dancing wildly.
At midnight, the captain blew the whistle.

As you learned earlier in this book, the subject of a sentence is the first noun or pronoun that is not part of a meaning unit (a group of words that work together as if they were one word). The subject is underlined in each of these sentences.

Aboard the ship, people were dancing wildly.
At midnight, the captain blew the whistle.

Both "ship" and "midnight" are nouns, but they belong to meaning units, in this case prepositional phrases. So neither can be the subject of the sentence. In the first sentence, "people" is the first noun that is not part of a meaning unit. In the second, "captain" is the first noun that is not part of a meaning unit.

Both of the prepositional phrases, even though they come at the beginning of the sentence, give further information about the verb. So each belongs to the verb, not to the subject.

Aboard the ship, [people] were dancing wildly.
At midnight, [the captain] blew the whistle.

As a rule, prepositional phrases that appear at the beginning of a sentence belong to the verb, not to the subject. Like other modifiers for verbs, they tell **when, why, how, or where**. "Aboard the ship" tells **where** the people were dancing. "At midnight" tells **when** the captain blew the whistle.

You might also notice that modifiers for the verb can be moved to the end of a sentence and still make sense.

People were dancing wildly **aboard the ship.**
The captain blew the whistle **at midnight.**

Exercise 2

In the sentences below, identify each prepositional phrase by circling the preposition, then underlining the rest of the phrase.

1. Augusta was married to a psychiatrist.

2. This psychiatrist loved Augusta despite her peculiarities.

3. Before their wedding, she wept for hours.

4. During the ceremony, she insisted on the presence of her African grey parrot, Marmaduke.

5. A bird with such a wide and colorful vocabulary can be an embarrassment.

6. It shouted at the minister.

7. It cursed during the vows.

8. Throughout the reception, it nibbled at the Waldorf salad.

9. These exotic birds live for forty to fifty years.

10. Despite this whole experience, the psychiatrist settled into marriage with Augusta.

Check your answers with the key at the end of the book.

Exercise 3

Now underline the subject once and the verb twice. Then bracket the subject cluster.

Keep in mind that prepositional phrases appearing at the beginning of a sentence generally belong to the verb, not to the subject.

1. Augusta was married to a psychiatrist.

2. This psychiatrist loved Augusta despite her peculiarities.

3. Before their wedding, she wept for hours.

4. During the ceremony, she insisted on the presence of her African grey parrot, Marmaduke.

5. A bird with such a wide and colorful vocabulary can be an embarrassment.

6. It shouted at the minister.

7. It cursed during the vows.

8. Throughout the reception, it nibbled at the Waldorf salad.

9. These exotic birds live for forty to fifty years.

10. Despite this whole experience, the psychiatrist settled into marriage with Augusta.

Check your answers with the key at the end of the book.

Present Participial Phrases

Another type of phrase modifier is the present participial phrase. This kind of meaning unit begins with an -ing form of a verb called the present participle: typing, fishing, thinking. You have seen present participles used as

1. Part of a sentence verb:

      HV   MV
  Tim was **planning** the trip.

      HV HV MV
  They will be **joining** us in Paris.

      HV HV   MV
  He had been **thinking** about the costs.

2. One-word modifiers:

  These **chirping** birds must go.
  You need a new **washing** machine.
  Working people need rest.

In function, present participial phrases resemble the one-word modifiers. They do not have helping verbs (was, will be, had been, etc.), so they cannot work as verbs. What they can do is modify some part of the sentence—in these examples, the subject.

  A man **wearing a plaid shirt** demanded all the money.

  Waving his fist, Jenkins frightened the other drivers.

  Jenkins, **waving his fist**, frightened the other drivers.

Both of these phrases describe the subject, so they belong to the subject cluster:

[A _man_ wearing a plaid shirt] <u>demanded</u> all the money.

[Waving his fist, <u>Jenkins</u>] <u>frightened</u> the other drivers.

[<u>Jenkins</u>, waving his fist,] <u>frightened</u> the other drivers.

As a rule, present participial phrases that occur directly before or after the subject belong to the subject.

On the other hand, to work as the verb of a sentence, rather than as a modifier, a participle must be preceded by one or more helping verbs:

           HV   MV
[The <u>man</u>] <u>was wearing</u> a plaid shirt.

            HV HV MV
[<u>Jenkins</u>] <u>had been waving</u> his fist at the other drivers.

Exercise 4

With the following sentences, underline the subject once and the verb twice. Then bracket the subject cluster. Put an HV over each helping verb, and an MV over each main verb.

1. Forcing her way, Belinda reached the autograph table of Margo Maven.

2. Belinda had been looking forward to this day.

3. Margo, glancing up at Belinda, suddenly frowned.

4. She was recalling Belinda's face.

5. Poor Belinda, just doing her job as a police officer, had ticketed the big star last week.

Check your answers with the key at the end of the book.

Past Participial Phrases

Past participial phrases are another type of meaning unit. These begin with a verb form called the past participle. Most past participles end in -ed: painted, baked, visited. Others end in -d, -en, -n, or -t: told, spoken, bent.

You have seen past participles used as

1. Part of a sentence verb:

> HV MV
> Bill has **baked** a cherry pie.

> HV   HV MV
> You should have **seen** the crowd.

> HV HV   MV
> The new Glitzmore Hotel will be **completed** in the spring.

2. One-word modifiers:

> A **trained** mechanic repaired my car.

> The **spoken** word can move people to action.

> Dorothy was **bored**.

Like one-word modifiers, past participial phrases work like adjectives to describe a noun or pronoun. In the above sentences, "trained" describes "mechanic," "spoken" describes "word," and "bored" describes "Dorothy."

Past participial phrases contain other modifiers, usually prepositional phrases.

> The mechanic, **trained in the latest automotive technology**, repaired our car in less than an hour.

> **Terrified of spiders**, Jamie refused to enter the old barn.

> **Frozen in ice**, the 2000 year-old man was perfectly preserved.

Notice that all of these past participial phrases **describe** nouns. They do not show what a noun **does**. In the first example "trained in the latest technology" describes the mechanic; it does not show what he did. The action is stated by the word "repaired." That's what the mechanic did: he repaired our car.

In each of these sentences, the past participial phrase modifies the subject so it belongs to the subject cluster:

> [The <u>mechanic</u>, trained in the latest automotive technology,] <u>repaired</u> our car in less than one hour.

> [Terrified of spiders, <u>Jamie</u>] <u>refused</u> to enter the old barn.

> [Frozen in ice, the 2000 year-old <u>man</u>] <u>was</u> perfectly preserved.

You may get confused when -ed forms come right after the subject. That's because an -ed form can also be the simple past tense of a verb. For example:

42

[The <u>mechanic</u>] <u>trained</u> our automotive students.

In this sentence, the -ed word tells what the mechanic **did**, so it is the verb of the sentence.

■ Reminders and Summary

1. The subject of a sentence is the first noun or pronoun that is not part of a meaning unit, a group of words that function like one word. So far, you have learned about three kinds of meaning units: prepositional phrases, present participial phrases, and past participial phrases.

2. The subject cluster consists of the subject plus all of its modifiers. These modifiers may be one-word modifiers as well as meaning units.

3. When an -ed form comes directly after a subject, ask whether it describes the subject or tells what the subject is doing. If the -ed form describes the subject, then it signals a past participial phrase and it belongs to the subject cluster. If the -ed form tells what the subject is doing, then it is the sentence verb.

Exercise 5

With these sentences, underline the subject once and the verb twice. Then bracket the subject cluster.

Examples:

[<u>Kittens</u> raised by their mother] <u>can survive</u> in the wilderness.

[The proud <u>mother</u>] <u>raised</u> her kittens.

1. Determined to win, Bernardo practiced the entire weekend.

2. Bernardo, determined to win, practiced the entire weekend.

3. An enthusiastic crowd filled the gym.

4. The crowd, filled with enthusiasm, cheered Bernardo.

5. A crowd filled with enthusiasm awaited his entrance.

Check your answers with the key at the end of the book.

Infinitive Phrases

As you learned in Chapter Two, infinitives consist of the word "to" followed by a verb form: to paint, to destroy, to win.

An infinitive phrase is a meaning unit that begins with an infinitive: to paint a house, to destroy the bridge, to win the lottery.

Like other meaning units, infinitive phrases can modify some part of a sentence. If an infinitive phrases modifies a noun or pronoun, it is functioning as an adjective. If an infinitive phrase modifies a verb, it is functioning as an adverb.

- **Infinitive Phrases That Function As Adjectives**

    The Olafson's struggle **to survive their first winter in America** impressed the townspeople.

In this sentence, "to survive their first winter in America" works as an adjective, telling what kind of struggle impressed the townspeople. The next sentence works in a similar way:

    The temptation **to quit work** was strong.

"To quit work" works as an adjective, telling what kind of temptation was strong.

Since both of these infinitive phrases modify the subject of the sentence they belong to the subject cluster:

    [The Olafson's <u>struggle</u> to survive their first winter in America] <u>impressed</u> the townspeople.

    [The <u>temptation</u> to quit work] <u>was</u> strong.

In other sentences, an infinitive phrase might modify a noun or pronoun that is not part of the subject cluster.

    [<u>Jenkins</u>] <u>made</u> many attempts **to contact his ex-wife.**

Here "to contact his ex-wife" works as an adjective, modifying the object of the sentence, "attempts." The infinitive phrase tells what kind of attempts:

- **Infinitive Phrases That Function as Adverbs**

    Jenkins hoped **to correct some misunderstandings.**

In this sentence "to correct some misunderstandings" works as an adverb, modifying the verb "hoped."

The next sentence works in a similar way:

Jenkins rushed **to answer the phone.**

Since both of the previous infinitive phrases modify the verb, they belong to the verb and not to the subject cluster:

[Jenkins] hoped to correct some misunderstandings.

[Jenkins] rushed to answer the phone.

Notice that these infinitive phrases modify the verb. They are not part of the verb itself.

Sometimes infinitive phrases that function as adverbs occur at the beginning of a sentence. These, too, belong to the verb and not to the subject cluster:

To correct some misunderstandings, Jenkins called his ex-wife.

"To correct some misunderstanding" does not describe Jenkins. Instead it tells why he called his ex-wife:

To correct some misunderstandings, [Jenkins] called his ex-wife.

Exercise 6

In these sentences, underline the subject once and the verb twice. Then bracket the subject cluster.

Examples:

[Alfredo's desire to marry a rich woman] forced him to join the country club.

To join this club, [he] had to sell his car.

1. O'Malley wanted to visit the ruins of ancient Egypt.

2. To get there, he had booked a flight to Cairo.

3. His plans to visit Luxor required an overnight train trip.

4. He had failed in earlier attempts to visit this cradle of civilization.

5. To assure success this time, O'Malley hired a reputable guide to oversee the entire adventure.

Check your answers with the key at the end of the book.

REVIEW

1. A meaning unit is a group of words that function like one word.

2. A phrase modifier is a type of meaning unit.

3. There are four kinds of phrase modifiers: prepositional phrases, present participial phrases, past participial phrases, and infinitive phrases.

4. A prepositional phrase begins with a small word that shows some kind of relationship (under, by, with, inside); a prepositional phrase ends with a noun (under the tree, by the river, with a dog, inside a house).

5. A prepositional phrase can function as either an adjective or an adverb.

6. A prepositional phrase usually follows the word it modifies (the **chair** under the tree, the **house** by the river). However prepositional phrases that occur at the very beginning of a sentence modify the verb, even though it appears later in the sentence.

7. Present and past participial phrases modify nouns or pronouns. Those that appear directly before or directly after the subject noun belong to the subject cluster.

8. Infinitive phrases consist of a verb form preceded by the word "to." They can function as either adjectives or adverbs.

9. An infinitive phrase, like an infinitive by itself, can never be the verb of a sentence.

10. An infinitive phrase at the very beginning of a sentence works like an adverb, so it belongs to the verb of the sentence and is not part of the subject cluster.

11. The subject of a sentence is the first noun or pronoun that is not part of a meaning unit.

Exercise 7

In the following sentences, underline the subject once and the verb twice. Then bracket the subject cluster. When finished, have an instructor or instructional assistant check your answers.

1. Before sunrise, Babette awoke to the sounds of bricks falling and wood splitting.

2. Peeking though the blinds, she saw the next door building being torn down.

3. She had checked into this quaint old inn to get some much needed sleep.

4. During her trip through Europe, she had found herself in one noisy hotel after another.

5. In Paris, she had stayed next door to a bakery.

6. The merry bakers, preparing croissants and baguettes, sang throughout the wee hours.

7. To get some sleep in Marseilles, she had taken a room above a night club.

8. Arriving in Rome, she checked into a little inn with rooms facing a courtyard.

9. This sweet little inn, protected from the street, seemed to offer some peace and quiet.

10. By 6:00 a.m., demolition crews had started their work.

Instrutor/Assistant Check _____

VI RECOGNIZING CLAUSE MODIFIERS

Clause modifiers are meaning units that contain their own subject and verb.

When the rain stopped, we left the cabin.

The subject of the sentence above is "we," and the verb is "left". However the clause modifier "when the rain stopped" also has a subject, "rain," and a verb, "stopped." The sentence below follows a similar pattern:

The man **who won last week's lottery** appeared on television last night.

In this sentence the subject is "man", and the verb is "appeared." However the clause modifier "who won last week's lottery" also has a subject, "who," and a verb, "won."

Like other meaning units, clause modifiers can function as either adjectives or adverbs. In the first sentence, "when the rain stopped" works like an adverb telling when we left the cabin. As a result it belongs to the verb.

When the rain stopped, [we] left the cabin.

In the second sentence, "who won last week's lottery" works like an adjective telling which man appeared on television last night. As a result it belongs to the subject cluster.

[The man who won last week's lottery] appeared on television last night.

You might also note that both sentences illustrate a general rule you have learned: The subject of a sentence is the first noun or pronoun that is not part of meaning unit.

Clause Modifiers That Belong To Verbs

Clause modifiers that tell when, why, or where, or that tell the condition under which something is done will modify verbs.

WHEN

After we ate the pizza, we started on the ice cream.

Before we left our apartment, we checked the windows and faucets.

Because we lost our credit cards, we called home for money.

Since we were afraid of alligators, we decided against swamp camping.

WHERE

Wherever we went, the hotel management seemed to watch us.

CONDITION

If you save money, you can afford a trip to New York.

Although we had no money, we checked into the very expensive Glitz-Royalton Hotel.

Like phrase modifiers, clause modifiers that refer to verbs can also appear at the end of a sentence and still make sense.

We started on the ice cream **after we finished the pizza.**
We checked the windows and faucets **before we left our apartment.**

We called home for money **because we lost our credit cards.**
We decided against swamp camping **because we were afraid of alligators.**

The hotel management seemed to watch us **wherever we went.**

You will not need to use your credit cards **if you save money.**
We checked into the Glitz-Royalton Hotel **although we had no money.**

These clause modifiers begin with a word or phrase called a **subordinator.** There are several subordinators:

after we finished the pizza
although no one had complained
as Martha left the office
as if you knew a better route
as long as we had some money
as though we were rich
because we won the game
before the show started
if you refuse to pay
in order that you drive safely
since we were afraid of alligators
so that we get there in time
that we had forgotten the canteen
though the food was terrible
till we find a better restaurant
unless Americans accept their new status

until we open our own place
when we arrive in Akron
whenever you make the decision
wherever we went
whereas the witness refused to appear
whether we win the case or not
while our attorneys discuss the matter

Exercise 1

In the following sentences, identify each clause modifier by circling the subordinator and then underlining the rest of the modifier.

Examples:

(Unless) someone watches me, I tend to lose things

(When) we arrived in Boston, I discovered (that) someone had taken my wallet.

1. Wherever we went, we were suspicious of everybody.

2. If others brushed close to us, we feared that they might be pickpockets.

3. After we had breakfast, we toured the Fine Arts Museum.

4. I felt safe as long as we stayed in the galleries.

5. Since art lovers are supposed to have solid values, we assumed that we had no problem.

6. As we walked into the new wing, we came upon a new exhibit called The Romance of Thievery.

7. Whether I was being paranoid or not, I felt threatened among these paintings of rosy-cheeked street urchins and bearded con-artists.

8. I became panicky whenever we saw anything connected with purse snatching.

9. When we finished the tour, I had developed a nervous twitch.

10. Some people remain nervous until they accept the basic insecurity of life.

Check your answers with the key at the end of the book.

Exercise 2

Now underline the subject once and the verb twice. Then put brackets around the subject cluster.

Remember the subject of a sentence is the first noun or pronoun that is not part of a meaning unit. Also remember that a clause modifier is one type of meaning unit.

Examples:

Unless someone watches me, [I] tend to lose things.

When we arrived in Boston, [I] discovered that someone had taken my wallet.

1. Wherever we went, we were suspicious of everybody.

2. If others brushed close to us, we feared that they might be pickpockets.

3. After we had breakfast, we toured the Fine Arts Museum.

4. I felt safe as long as we stayed in the galleries.

5. Since art lovers are supposed to have solid values, we assumed that we had no problem.

6. As we walked into the new wing, we came upon a new exhibit called The Romance of Thievery.

7. Whether I was being paranoid or not, I felt threatened among these paintings of rosy-cheeked street urchins and bearded con-artists.

8. I became panicky whenever we saw anything connected with purse snatching.

9. When we finished the tour, I had developed a nervous twitch.

10. Some people remain nervous until they accept the basic insecurity of life.

Check your answers with the key at the end of the book.

Clause Modifiers That Belong To Nouns Or Pronouns

These clause modifiers—usually beginning with the subordinators "who," "which," "that," or "where" —point directly back to a noun or pronoun, working like adjectives to modify that noun or pronoun.

> The cat **that ate the canary** looked guilty but satisfied.

> The canary belonged to a woman **who despised cats.**

> Her first canary, **which she cherished as her great friend in life,** had suffered the same fate.

> These sad events were famous in the town **where she lived.**

Clause modifiers have their own subject and verb. In the first sentence, the subordinator "that" functions as the subject for the verb "ate." In the second sentence, the subordinator "who" functions as the subject for the verb "despised." In the third, the pronoun "she" is the subject for the verb "cherished." In the last, the pronoun "she" is the subject for the verb "lived."

But like all clause modifiers, these clause modifiers do not contain the subject and verb of the sentence. Instead they modify some part of the subject cluster or verb cluster.

In the first sentence, "that ate the canary" modifies the subject "cat," telling which cat. In the second, the modifier "who despised cats" describes the word "woman," telling which woman. In the third, the modifier "which she cherished as her great friend in life" refers to the subject "canary," giving us more information about the canary. In the last, the modifier "where she lived" identifies the town.

Clause modifiers that modify some part of the subject cluster belong to the subject cluster. Those that modify some part of the verb cluster belong to the verb cluster.

> [The <u>cat</u> that ate the canary] <u>looked</u> guilty but satisfed.

> [The <u>canary</u>] <u>belonged</u> to a woman who despised cats.

> [Her first <u>canary</u>, which she cherished as her great friend in life] <u>had</u> <u>suffered</u> the same fate.

> [These sad <u>events</u>] <u>were</u> famous in the town where she lived.

Expanded Clause Modifiers

Sometimes a noun as well as one or more adjectives are included at the beginning of a who, which, that or where clause:

James Muskrat, **a pioneer** who paddled up the whitewater of the Skeedaddle River, was honored at the Manitou County Fair.

Muskratville, **a sleepy little town** that rarely makes the news, welcomed television crews from the networks.

The noun points back to the noun it modifies, which in these two sentences is the subject:

[James Muskrat, a pioneer who paddled up the whitewaters of the Skeedaddle River,] was honored at the Manitou County Fair.

[Muskratville, a sleepy little town that rarely makes the news,] welcomed television crews from the networks.

Such an expanded clause modifier may also appear **before** the subject of the sentence:

A pioneer who paddled up the whitewaters of the Skeedaddle River, James Muskrat was honored at the Manitou County Fair.

A sleepy little town that rarely makes the news, Muskratville welcomed television crews from the networks.

With these expanded clause modifiers, a noun appears before the subordinator. However this additional noun, being part of a meaning unit, will not be the subject of the sentence. As you have learned, the subject will be the first noun or pronoun that is not part of a meaning unit:

[A pioneer who paddled up the whitewaters of the Skeedaddle River, James Muskrat] was honored at the Manitou County Fair.

[A sleepy little town that rarely makes the news, Muskratville] welcomed television crews from the networks.

Exercise 3

In the following sentences, identify each clause modifier by circling the introductory word **(who, which, that, where)** , then underlining the rest of the modifier.

Examples:

My uncle (who) <u>lives in Tulsa</u> has married for the fourth time.

My uncle, <u>a man</u> (who) <u>truly loves life</u>, has married for the fourth time.

<u>A man</u> (who) <u>truly loves life</u>, my uncle has married for the fourth time.

1. The town where my cousins live is filled with generous if eccentric millionaires.

2. Those who like to be around big money and unusual people would love the place.

3. Patricia Hernandez, a big-hearted woman who loves animals, has contributed over $500,000 to the care of stray cats.

4. These cats that she supports have grown to be plump, beautiful, and demanding.

5. Jim Hawkins, who made his money on strawberry preserves, supports the town's Museum of Jams and Jellies.

6. The nation's only museum that features spreadable sweets, this institution attracts tourists from all parts of the country.

7. Marmalandia, which opened last year, is its most popular exhibit.

8. Otis Blinker, a feisty industrialist who once arm wrestled Edsel Ford, financed the town's architectural centerpiece, a 10-story bell tower that tolls on the hour.

9. A man who loves anything that rings, Blinker visits the tower regularly.

10. His favorite bar, which is located across the street, allows him to savor many a concert.

Check your answers with the key at the end of the book.

Exercise 4

Now underline the subject once and the verb twice. Then put brackets around the subject cluster.

Remember the subject of a sentence is the first noun or pronoun that is not part of a meaning unit. Also remember that a clause modifier is one type of meaning unit.

Examples:

[My <u>uncle</u> who lives in Tulsa] <u>has married</u> for the fourth time.

[My <u>uncle</u>, a man who truly loves life,] <u>has married</u> for the fourth time.

[A man who truly loves life, my <u>uncle</u>] <u>has married</u> for the fourth time.

1. The town where my cousins live is filled with generous if eccentric millionaires.

2. Those who like to be around big money and unusual people would love the place.

3. Patricia Hernandez, a big-hearted woman who loves animals, has contributed over $500,000 to the care of stray cats.

4. These cats that she supports have grown to be plump, beautiful, and demanding.

5. Jim Hawkins, who made his money on strawberry preserves, supports the town's Museum of Jams and Jellies.

6. The nation's only museum that features spreadable sweets, this institution attracts tourists from all parts of the country.

7. Marmalandia, which opened last year, is its most popular exhibit.

8. Otis Blinker, a feisty industrialist who once arm wrestled Edsel Ford, financed the town's architectural centerpiece, a 10-story bell tower that tolls on the hour.

9. A man who loves anything that rings, Blinker visits the tower regularly.

10. His favorite bar, which is located across the street, allows him to savor many a concert.

Check your answers with the key at the end of the book.

Review

1. A clause modifier is a meaning unit which has its own subject and verb.

2. The subject and verb of a meaning unit will never be the subject and verb of a sentence.

3. Like other modifiers, clause modifiers can function as either adverbs or adjectives.

4. Clause modifiers that function as adverbs begin with subordinators like these: although, since, when, because, if, while. They tell when, where, how, or why, or they tell the condition under which something is done. These clause modifiers modify verbs.

5. Clause modifiers that refer to the verb can usually be moved to the end of a sentence and still make sense.

6. Clause modifiers that function as adjectives begin with subordinators like who, which, that, and where. They further identify a noun or pronoun. If this kind of clause modifier refers to the subject, then it belongs to the subject cluster.

7. Sometimes a noun as well as one or more adjectives are included at the beginning of a who, which, that or where clause.

Exercise 5

In the following sentences, underline the subject once and bracket the subject cluster. When you are finished, have an instructor or instructional assistant check your answers.

1. While King Rupert's palace guards slept in the tower, Bengar's enemy forces were gathering across the Kline River.

2. People who had never seen King Rupert were amazed at his long red hair and toothless grin.

3. When news of the threat reached the king, he hastily gathered an army of untrained and unwilling peasants.

4. Those who volunteered were expecting a solid meal.

5. Although the king had raised 500 troops by noon, he had neglected to prepare for lunch.

6. Since the troops knew their rights, Rupert faced rebellion and desertion.

7. A resourceful man who knew his way around the palace, Rupert raided the royal pantry.

8. A banquet, which consisted of pheasant and brandied fruit, lifted the mens' spirits and gave them the strength that they needed for battle.

9. Leaders who want to win must remember the hearts, minds, and stomachs of their soldiers.

10. King Rupert, a wise old veteran who had seen many a battle, wept as he watched his lusty troops march toward the Kline.

Instructor/Assistant Check: _____

VII REVIEW AND SENTENCE VARIATIONS

■ ■ Meaning Unit Review
■ ■
■

You now have some basic tools to help you read sentences with more accuracy and ease. Central among these tools is the ability to identify the first noun or pronoun that is not part of a meaning unit. When you have found this first noun or pronoun, you have recognized the subject of a sentence.

To identify the first noun or pronoun that is not part of meaning unit, you must be able to recognize meaning units. In much of this book, that is what you have been learning to do. You have learned that there are six types of meaning units:

Prepositional Phrases: by the old mill stream, during the night, to the corner store

Infinitive Phrases: to bake a pie, to quit a bad job, to feed the hamsters

Present Participial Phrases: holding the baby, realizing the danger, cleaning the oven

Past Participial Phrases: terrified of snakes, shocked at Jennifer's behavior, caught in a blizzard

Clause Modifiers for Verbs: when Jon walked in the door, because the refrigerator was empty, if you want to have dinner

Clause Modifiers for Nouns and Pronouns: who saved a great deal of money, which threatened the village, that shrieked in the night, where we travelled each summer

The ablility to recognize meaning units is particularly important when they appear directly before the subject:

During the night [a few <u>campers</u>] <u>were frightened</u> by animal noises.

[Terrified of snakes, <u>Bill</u>] <u>avoided</u> the swamp tour.

[Realizing the danger, the <u>studio</u>] <u>hired</u> a stunt specialist.

Because the refrigerator was empty, [<u>he</u>] <u>called</u> Pizza Express.

By recognizing these introductory word groups as meaning units, you know that any nouns they contain will not be the subject. Instead look for the first noun or pronoun that is not part of a meaning unit. That noun or pronoun will be the subject.

Also important is to recognize those meaning units that come directly after the subject:

[The <u>house</u> by the old mill stream] <u>belongs</u> to Edith Berlucci.

"By the old mill stream" is a prepositional phrase telling which house, so it belongs to the subject cluster. The verb cluster begins with the the verb itself, "belongs."

Here is another example:

[The <u>house</u> that Sutter built] now <u>belongs</u> to the state.

"That Sutter built" is a clause modifier telling which house, so it is a part of the subject cluster. The verb cluster begins with the adverb "now."

By recognizing these meaning units, you can tell where the subject cluster ends.

 # Exercise 1

In these sentences, identify each meaning unit by circling the word that signals the beginning of a meaning unit. Then underline the rest of the meaning unit. Remember that meaning units can often appear inside other meaning units.

Examples:

The house (that) <u>we bought</u> was built in <u>1907</u>.

(During) <u>our first year</u>, we hope (to) <u>restore the front porch</u>.

The previous owners, (determined) <u>to look modern</u>, had added aluminum siding (to) <u>the whole place</u>.

(In) <u>the eight years</u> (that) <u>the Camerons had lived</u> (in) Boise, they had never visited the zoo.

1. Mt. Lassen, which is a 10,453 foot volcano located fifty miles east of Redding, California, last erupted in 1917.

2. Mt. Lassen, a volcano located fifty miles east of Redding, California, last erupted in 1917.

3. Lassen belongs to the Circle of Fire, which is a series of volcanoes that ring the Pacific Ocean.

4. About 11,000 years ago, while glaciers still covered this area, a one-cubic mile dome of semi-solid lava thrust from the earth.

5. In 1917, an endless flow of steaming lava, undeterred by the overlying rock, devastated the mountainside.

6. Moving ever forward, the lava toppled great stands of old-growth forest.

7. Over two hundred miles away, San Franciscans were shocked to see the sky darken.

8. Today, Lassen National Park is one of the least known of the National Parks.

9. Although steam was still visible in summit craters until the early 1940's, only thin wisps appear today.

10. But in one part of the park, steaming fumeroles give evidence of the power that remains under the ground.

Check your answers with the key at the end of the book.

Exercise 2

Now that you have identified the meaning units, you can recognize the subject and verb.

In each sentence, underline the subject once and the verb twice. Then bracket the subject cluster.

1. Mt. Lassen, which is a 10,453 foot volcano located fifty miles east of Redding, California, last erupted in 1917.

2. Mt. Lassen, a volcano located fifty miles east of Redding, California, last erupted in 1917.

3. Lassen belongs to the Circle of Fire, which is a series of volcanoes that ring the Pacific Ocean.

4. About 11,000 years ago, while glaciers still covered this area, a one-cubic mile dome of semi-solid lava thrust from the earth.

5. In 1917, an endless flow of steaming lava, undeterred by the overlying rock, devastated the mountainside.

6. Moving ever forward, the lava toppled great stands of old-growth forest.

7. Over two hundred miles away, San Franciscans were shocked to see the sky darken.

8. Today, Lassen National Park is one of the least known of the National Parks.

9. Although steam was still visible in summit craters until the early 1940's, only thin wisps appear today.

10. But in one part of the park, steaming fumeroles give evidence of the power that remains under the ground.

Check your answers with the key at the end of the book.

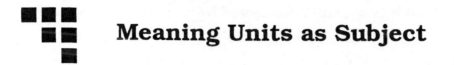

Meaning Units as Subject

As a rule, the subject of a sentence is the first noun or pronoun that is not part of a meaning unit. However you will find some sentences that follow a different pattern. For example:

Waiting in an airport can be frustrating.

In this sentence, there is no noun or pronoun outside of the introductory meaning unit "waiting in an airport." In such a sentence, the entire meaning unit functions as the subject.

The pattern would be represented like this:

[Waiting in an airport] can be frustrating.

The next sentence follows a similar pattern:

To complete a college degree is a major achievement.

Again there is no noun or pronoun outside of the meaning unit. Consequently the meaning unit itself is the subject:

[To complete a college degree] is a major achievement.

We can now state a new rule to allow for sentences following this pattern: If there is no noun or pronoun outside of a meaning unit then the entire meaning unit will be the subject of a sentence.

When using this rule, however, you must be careful not to jump to conclusions. If there is a noun or a pronoun outside of a meaning unit, then that first noun or pronoun serves as the subject.

[Waiting in the airport, Damian] became tired and frustrated.

OR

To complete his college degree, [he] took additional courses in the summer.

So far you have seen two types of meaning units that can function as the subject of a sentence: **present participial phrases** and **infinitive phrases.**

However, **clauses** can also function as the subject of a sentence. These clauses typically begin with **that, whoever,** or **whichever:**

[That women can be heads of state] can hardly be denied.

[Whoever rang the firebell] is in big trouble.

[Whichever hotel you choose] is fine with me.

Exercise 3

In each of the following sentences, underline the subject once and the verb twice. Then bracket the subject cluster.

1. To get rich was Martha's lifelong goal.

2. To win the lottery, she bought $100 worth of tickets each payday.

3. Whoever wins the lottery will live well for years to come.

4. That Martha knew this was clear to us all.

5. Winning 10 million dollars would allow her to jet around the world and to eat whatever she wanted.

6. Hoping to be the first millionaire in her family, Martha had speculated in real estate.

7. To get started, she purchased a tiny cabin in Virginia.

8. Unfortunately, repairing an old log cabin takes skill and money.

9. At the end of two years, the cabin had become home to a family of skunks.

10. To clear them out would have cost considerable effort and money.

Check your answers with the key at the end of the book.

Quotes – Direct and Indirect

When you **directly** quote someone, you give their exact words and enclose them in quotation marks.

> Busby said, "The time has come to start anew."

Strictly speaking, the subject of the sentence is "Busby" and the verb is "said." However when you are referring to what someone has said, you are more interested in what it is they said:

> Busby said, "[The time] has come to start anew."

The same is true even if you do not use the exact words of the person you are quoting:

> Busby said we should start over again.

Even though you are quoting Busby **indirectly**, you are still interested in what he said:

Busby said [we] <u>should start over</u> again.

With some indirect quotes, the name of the speaker may not be indicated:

The weather reports said that [a <u>blizzard</u>] <u>is coming</u>.

It is reported that [the <u>pilot</u>] <u>pulled</u> the wrong lever.

With quotes, whether they are direct or indirect, you are normally more interested in what is said rather than who said it. Therefore, look for the subject in the quoted part of the sentence.

Exercise 4

In each of the following sentences, underline the subject once and the verb twice. Then bracket the subject cluster. These sentences contain direct and indirect quotes.

1. The newspapers said that Senator Methuselah had slept throughout the entire congressional session.

2. It is thought that Methuselah is over 100 years old.

3. Senator Ratchet said the ancient legislator was acquainted with Theodore Roosevelt.

4. Andrea Bernstein once wrote: "Senator Methuselah is our connection with history, our touchstone with the nation's founders."

5. Methuselah believes that we should reelect Grover Cleveland.

Check your answers with the key at the end of the book.

Sentences Beginning with "There"

When the word "there" appears at the beginning of a sentence, the subject will appear after rather than before the verb:

There <u>are</u> [too many <u>people</u>] in this poorly ventilated room.

The usual subject-verb pattern would be:

[Too many <u>people</u>] <u>are</u> in this poorly ventilated room.

In some sentences beginning with "there," the subject cluster will come between the helping verb and the main verb:

There <u>were</u> [several <u>bullets</u>] <u>lying</u> in the desk drawer.

The usual subject-verb pattern would be:

[Several <u>bullets</u>] <u>were lying</u> in the desk drawer.

In any case, the word "there" is not the subject of the sentence.

Exercise 5

In each of the following sentences, underline the subject once and the verb twice. Then bracket the subject cluster.

1. There were 50,000 people at the Gloomray concert.

2. There was a hard-core crowd at the foot of the stage.

3. There were a few enthusiastic fans holding up sequin-covered signs that welcomed Gloomray.

4. There was deafening applause when Gloomray strutted onto the stage.

5. There was a 300-pound security guard standing at the stage door.

Multiple Subjects and Verbs

Sometimes a sentence has more than one subject.

[<u>Brenda</u> and <u>Richard</u>] <u>were</u> childhood sweethearts.

[<u>Reading maps</u> and <u>tuning the radio</u>] <u>can be</u> dangerous when driving.

[<u>Planes</u>, <u>trains</u>, and <u>buses</u>] <u>can destroy</u> the nerves of a weary traveller.

In the same way, a sentence can have more than one verb.

[<u>Richard</u>] <u>called</u> Brenda and <u>asked</u> her to marry him.

[Her <u>mother</u> and <u>father</u>] <u>learned</u> about the proposal and <u>became</u> furious.

[<u>Leaving the proposal on voice mail</u>] <u>had shocked</u> and <u>irritated</u> them.

Review

1. Usually the subject of a sentence will be the first noun or pronoun that is not part of a meaning unit.

2. If there is no noun or pronoun outside of a meaning unit, then the entire meaning unit may be the subject.

3. If a sentence features a direct or indirect quote, the subject will appear inside the quote.

4. When "there" appears at the beginning of a sentence, the subject will follow the verb.

5. A sentence may have more than one subject and more than one verb.

Exercise 6

In the following sentences, underline the subject once and the verb twice. (Remember some sentences may have more than one subject and verb.) Then bracket the subject cluster.

When you are finished, have an instructor or instructional assistant check your answers.

1. Shortly before midnight on April 14, 1912, the legendary Titanic collided with an iceberg off the coast of Newfoundland.

2. After only two hours and forty minutes, the magnificent new liner went down with a loss of more than 1,500 lives.

3. The root cause of this catastrophe, which was reported as the worst ship wreck in history, was simply bad seamanship.

4. Despite all the iceberg warnings, the ship's officers insisted on full-speed.

5. Believing the ship was unsinkable, they felt secure.

6. Believing the ship unsinkable was a fatal mistake.

7. Passengers and crew scrambled for the life boats.

8. They hurriedly uncovered the boats and lowered them to the icy water below.

9. To survive such an ordeal required physical strength and emotional fortitude.

10. That they would be rescued was not certain.

■ In the remaining sentences, <u>underline the subject only</u>.

1. The Zoo Guide said that penguins do not always live in cold places.

2. There is one penguin species that lives right on the equator where it can be quite hot.

3. It goes on to say that some penguins live on islands.

4. As you may know, there are zoos which feature penguins as performers.

5. The Guide also said that these flightless birds do not live at the North Pole.

Instructor/Assistant Check: _____

PRACTICE SENTENCES I

Directions: Underline the subject once and the verb twice. Then bracket the subject cluster. When you are finished, have an instructor or instructional assistant check your answers.

1. *Life* magazine once listed 100 people who have made America great.

2. While all of these individuals have lived during the Twentieth Century, many are not household names.

3. Wallace Carothers, an Iowa chemist who worked for Du Pont, invented nylon and other synthetics.

4. Another great contributor to the American way of living is Willis Carrier.

5. Carrier, who lived in upstate New York, thought up the principle of air-conditioning while driving his family to church.

6. Obsessed with this idea, he made a u-turn and returned home.

7. According to his son, they never made it to church that day.

8. Air-conditioning is to a great extent responsible for the tremendous growth of America's sun-belt, areas such as Florida, Texas, Arizona, New Mexico, and parts of California.

9. Master Card and VISA fans can give thanks to an even lesser known American named Frank McNamara.

10. After dining out with friends and realizing he didn't have enough cash to pay the bill, McNamara invented the Diner's Club.

11. Its members could use the card in a variety of establishments.

12. While card holders have loved these services, paying the monthly balance has become a problem.

13. To avoid paying interest, they must pay the entire amount.

14. *Life* did not mention Philo T. Farnsworth, an Idaho farm boy who came to be regarded as the inventor of television.

15. In 1930, Farnsworth developed an electronic scanning system that made television viewing suitable for the home.

16. A statue of Farnsworth, with a cathode ray tube in hand, now stands in the United States Capitol, just to the right of Dr. Martin Luther King.

17. Other scientists contributed to the refinement of this revolutionary technology.

18. In 1936, the tempo of television's development quickened.

19. RCA began field tests of an all-electronic system from the Empire State Building.

20. Offering twice-a-week broadcasts, RCA established scheduled television.

21. During the 1950's, television became a way of life in America.

22. For children, Saturday morning meant the *Howdy Doody Show*, which featured a freckle-faced puppet and a mischievous clown named Clarabelle.

23. The first big hit was NBC's *Texaco Star Theater*, a variety show starring comedian Milton Berle.

24. That Berle was the king of comedy was unquestioned.

25. From 1948 to 1958, most TV programming was live.

26. Variety shows, dramas, and game shows originated in the studio.

27. As a result, bloopers were a regular part of television viewing.

28. People spilled coffee, tripped over each other, and said outrageous things.

29. Elvis Presley, soon to become the King of Rock and Roll, appeared on the *Ed Sullivan Show*.

30. The show's producers, fearing that the public would be shocked by Presley's swiveling hips, instructed camera operators to aim above the belt.

Directions: In each of these sentences, simply underline the subject.

1. In 1948, there were 36 television stations on the air.

2. Many believed that television was the plaything of the wealthy.

3. According to many historians, the war in Korea (1950-1953) delayed television's further development.

4. There were three networks in 1955: NBC, CBS, and ABC.

5. Analysts believe that the network system is fighting for its life, largely because of cable television's spectacular growth.

Instructor/Assistant Check: _____

PRACTICE SENTENCES II

Directions: Underline the subject once and the verb twice. Then bracket the subject cluster. When you are finished, have an instructor or instructional assistant check your answers.

1. Film makers achieve much of their magic through a variety of special effects.

2. The 1933 film *King Kong* was one of the first to include such wizardry.

3. In one scene, the young heroine, tied between two pillars in the center of a jungle, shrieks as a giant ape approaches her.

4. With one finger, he loosens her bonds as she continues to scream and struggle.

5. Having freed her, he picks her up with a Volkswagen-sized paw and lumbers into the wilderness.

6. For most of this scene, the ape was a model, only 18 inches high.

7. To achieve the desired effect, technicians projected film of the ape and the jungle set onto the back of a translucent screen.

8. Fay Wray, who played the heroine, acted out her role in front of the screen.

9. This method, which has been improved over the years, is called back or rear projection,

10. Making the miniatures for films is no small task.

11. The model battleships used in *Tora Tora Tora*, a film about the bombing of Pearl Harbor, were 40 feet long.

12. In *Close Encounters of the Third Kind*, the Indiana landscape over which flying saucers appeared consisted of miniature houses less than one-inch high.

13. Explosions and fires require various techniques and contraptions.

14. Sometimes movie makers actually burn a real building.

15. To produce an impressive fire, they often use the "Dante" machine, a device consisting of a car engine, a pump, and two 50-gallon drums of fuel.

16. This fire machine can create a 60-foot-wide wall of fire.

17. These clever techniques have brought incredible levels of realism to the movies.

71

18. The film *Alien* remains a gripping experience.

19. The crew of a space ship lands on a distant planet where a colony has mysteriously been destroyed.

20. One crew member, played by John Hurt, bends over to examine a peculiar object submerged in a watery cavern.

21. In a terrifying second, a crustacean-like creature attacks him, fastening itself to his face.

22. Later, on board the ship, they can find no trace of the creature on or near Hurt.

23. The dinner scene, however, reveals where the creature had concealed itself.

24. After Hurt finishes coughing violently, a jaw-snapping creature bursts from his chest.

25. Their appetites ruined, the other crew members run from the table.

26. To find and capture the alien was virtually impossible.

27. With each scene, it changed its form and emerged from a new place.

28. Scouring every corridor of the ship, the crew searched for the dread monster.

29. Turning a corner could prove fatal.

30. Actually the creature was nothing more than a cleverly fashioned puppet.

Directions: In each of these sentences, simply underline the subject.

1. The newspapers said that *Gorgon the Gobbler* was the most horrifying movie ever made.

2. There was a rumor that Gorgon would consume the entire cast.

3. There were over 500 people in the theater, gripping the arms of their chairs.

4. It was reported that ten people fainted during the first twenty minutes.

5. Some say a nurse trained in horror movie medicine treated them in the lobby.

Instructor/Assistant Check: _____

Some of the special effects examples in Practice Sentences II are based on data supplied in How in the World? Pleasantville, NY: Reader's Digest Association. 1990. pp. 406–414.

KEY TO EXERCISES

Exercise

1. The next door <u>neighbors</u> <u>dance</u> late at night.

2. Our computer store <u>manager</u> <u>is improving</u> the business.

3. At sunrise, 10,000 Yosemite <u>campers</u> <u>ran</u> for the showers.

4. Ben's old <u>Buick</u>, far too big for the garage, <u>had faded</u> from years in the hot sun.

5. <u>Denims</u> purchased at Frank's Big and Tall <u>will shrink</u> after the first washing.

6. <u>Chad</u> <u>sold</u> the Porsche to his now prosperous ex-wife.

7. Bernie's once famous <u>restaurant</u> <u>had become</u> nothing more than a hashhouse with a fancy menu.

8. The <u>veal</u> baked in heavy cream <u>is</u> my favorite dish.

9. Bernie's house <u>special</u> <u>is</u> shark steak with jellied Moray eel.

10. *For Whom the Bell Tolls* <u>is</u> a novel set during the Spanish Civil War.

 ## Chapter One

Exercise 1

1. The <u>heart</u> is an <u>organ</u> which is difficult to replace. (Both words name; both words are preceded by a determiner.)

2. <u>Forests</u> are vital to our <u>environment</u>. (Both of the underlined words name.)

3. The <u>computer</u> has become a <u>necessity</u> in most <u>offices.</u> (Each of the underlined words names; the first two underlined words are preceded by determiners; the last word, <u>offices</u>, is plural.)

4. <u>Dennis</u> knows the <u>cure</u> for your <u>difficulties</u>. (Each of the underlined words names; <u>cure</u> is preceded by a determiner; <u>difficulties</u> is plural.)

5. <u>Chicago</u> is famous for its <u>architecture</u>. (Each of the underlined words names. <u>Chicago</u> is the name of a place, <u>architecture</u> the name of an idea—in this case, a type of art.)

6. The <u>work</u> is too dangerous. (<u>Work</u> names an activity; it is preceded by a determiner.)

7. <u>Seattle</u> offers great <u>views</u>. (<u>Seattle</u> is the name of a place; <u>views</u> is the name of a generalized thing; here, <u>views</u> is plural.

8. A great <u>view</u> can cost <u>money</u>. (<u>View</u> takes a determiner here; <u>money</u> is the name of a thing.

9. <u>Anxiety</u> is a general <u>uneasiness</u>. (Both <u>anxiety</u> and <u>uneasiness</u> name a feeling; both can take a determiner.)

10. The <u>view</u> from our cheap <u>room</u> was a <u>disappointment</u>. (<u>Room</u> names a thing, can take a determiner, and can be singular or plural; <u>disappointment</u> names a feeling, takes a determiner, and can be singular or plural.)

Exercise 2

1. <u>They</u> walked in quietly, hoping the teacher wouldn't see <u>them</u>.

2. <u>Something</u> was bothering <u>him</u>.

3. <u>Anyone</u> is welcome to come to the concert.

4. <u>Somebody</u> had called the police.

5. During the night, <u>we</u> heard <u>them</u> shouting.

Exercise 3

1. <u>Connections</u> are quite useful.

2. The <u>blintzes</u> were delicious.

3. *Star Wars* is a movie about good and evil.

4. <u>Something</u> always goes wrong.

5. The <u>peak</u> of Mt. Ranier is visible from Seattle.

6. The <u>environment</u> has become increasingly important to us.

7. <u>Robert Stack</u> played the role of Elliot Ness in the television series *The Untouchables*.

8. <u>He</u> was a confident, matter-of-fact agent for the FBI.

9. <u>That</u> was just fine.

10. <u>Anyone</u> with money is welcome to come.

Chapter Two

Exercise 1

1. Our school principal wore ugly suits.

   (MV over "wore")

2. Our school principal has often worn ugly suits.

   (HV over "has", MV over "worn")

3. Everyone in our family has a cold.

   (MV over "has")

4. My Uncle Homer was a farmer in downstate Illinois.

   (MV over "was")

5. Uncle Homer was milking the cows at daybreak.

   (HV over "was", MV over "milking")

6. We must have danced all night.

   (HV HV over "must have", MV over "danced")

7. I was a bus driver in Chicago.

   (MV over "was")

8. I was driving an express on the near north side.

   (HV over "was", MV over "driving")

9. You might have called me first.

   (HV HV over "might have", MV over "called")

10. Terry has been playing the saxophone since childhood.

    (HV HV over "has been", MV over "playing")

Exercise 2

1. Dr. Salk wanted to find a polio vaccine.

   (MV over "wanted", INF over "to find")

2. Dr. Sabin was looking for an oral vaccine.

   (HV over "was", MV over "looking")

3. Parents tried to comfort their children.

   (MV over "tried", INF over "to comfort")

4. The nurses were hoping to avoid a strike.

   (HV over "were", MV over "hoping", INF over "to avoid")

5. Their union had been working on a contract.

   (HV HV over "had been", MV over "working")

Exercise 3

1. <u>Jessica</u> <u>was working</u> at Bloomingdale's.

2. <u>She</u> <u>had wanted</u> to be a movie star.

3. Some <u>people</u> <u>are</u> dreamers.

4. <u>They</u> <u>are dreaming</u> of better times in better cities.

5. <u>Reading</u> <u>requires</u> an active mind.

6. An estimated 50,000 <u>bees</u> <u>swarmed</u> into a subway station in Rio de Janeiro.

7. <u>They</u> <u>attacked</u> passengers on platforms and in trains.

8. Apparently a <u>tractor</u> <u>had disturbed</u> the beehive.

9. <u>Insects</u> <u>have been known</u> to change people's lives.

10. <u>Termites</u> <u>have devoured</u> house, home, and an occasional shopping mall.

◼◼◼
◼◼ Chapter Three
◼

Exercise 1

    ADJ   ADJ
1. [Nosy <u>neighbors</u>] <u>can cause</u> big problems.

    ADJ   ADV   ADJ
2. [Disposal <u>trucks</u>] sometimes <u>awaken</u> light sleepers.

       ADV
3. [<u>We</u>] desperately <u>wanted</u> to complain.

       ADJ
4. [The local <u>authorities</u>] <u>ignored</u> us.

                        ADJ
5. [The <u>mayor</u>] <u>had been reading</u> environmental reports.

       ADV
6. [<u>Olivier</u>] finally <u>left</u> the stage.

                ADJ
7. [The <u>Romans</u>] <u>wanted</u> to rule the whole world.

     ADJ
8. [<u>They</u>] <u>built</u> a complex infrastructure.

              ADJ
9. [It] <u>included</u> vast roadways and aqueducts.

       ADJ   ADV
10. [Some <u>aqueducts</u>] still <u>stand</u>.

Exercise 2

     ADJ   ADJ   ADJ
1. [Our camping <u>trip</u>] <u>was</u> a real adventure.

2. [We] <u>had forgotten</u> to bring the cooler.

     ADJ   ADJ
3. [Car <u>sickness</u>] <u>was</u> a family trait.

        ADV   ADJ   ADJ
4. Eventually [the car's radiator <u>hose</u>] <u>broke</u>.

                ADJ
5. [Aunt Pearl] <u>told</u> corny jokes.

       ADJ   ADJ   ADJ
6. [The camp <u>ground</u>] <u>was</u> noisy and crowded.

   ADJ ADJ   ADJ   ADJ   ADV
7. [Our poor <u>dog</u>, flea-bitten and nervous,] <u>whined</u> continuously.

     ADJ   ADJ ADJ   ADJ
8. [Horton's <u>store</u>] <u>had sold</u> its last bottle of mosquito repellent.

        ADJ   ADJ   ADV
9. [The <u>kids</u>, bored and itchy,] <u>fought</u> incessantly.

     ADV   ADJ ADJ
10. Amazingly [we] <u>survived</u> our dream vacation.

Chapter Four

Exercise 1

            PN
1. [Snakes] <u>are</u> reptiles.

           LV   **PA**
2. [Some <u>snakes</u>] <u>are</u> famous.

          HV LV   **PA**
3. [Pythons] <u>have been</u> notorious.

                            AV   **OBJ**
4. [These large <u>snakes</u>] <u>consume</u> sizeable animals.

           HV   AV   **OBJ**
5. [A <u>Python</u>] <u>can swallow</u> a forty-pound pig.

                                 AV   **OBJ**
6. [A 16-foot African rock <u>python</u>] once <u>ate</u> a 130-pound impala.

                            AV
7. Afterwards, [the sated <u>snake</u>] <u>relaxes</u>. **(There is no object, predicate adjective, or predicate noun in this sentence.)**

                      HV LV **PA**
8. [The python's feeding <u>habits</u>] <u>can be</u> irregular.

                  HV AV   **OBJ**
9. Annually [a <u>python</u>] <u>may eat</u> only eight meals.

            LV   **PN**
10. Clearly [this <u>snake</u>] <u>is</u> no pig.

Exercise 2

          LV
1. Tim had **been** the boss previously.

              LV
2. Unfortunately Tim **was** insensitive.

             HV
3. The secretaries **were** always complaining about him.

      HV
4. He **was** always forgetting their birthdays.

          LV
5. Birthdays **are** important to most people.

        HV
6. He had **been** trying to remember them.

        LV
7. But he **was** hopeless.

        HV
8. He **was** neglecting everyone's special day.

LV
9. Tanya **was** aware of his shortcomings.

LV
10. Soon birthday parties **were** her trademark.

Exercise 3

LV
1. Rose **appeared** lost.

LV
2. She **looked** dizzy.

AV
3. We had **looked** for her all morning.

LV
4. Earlier she had **felt** ill.

AV
5. Denna **felt** Rose's pulse.

Chapter Five

Exercise 1

1. (At) daybreak, Yvette was preparing (for) Augusta's visit.

2. She dragged the vacuum cleaner (up) the stairs and (into) the guest room.

3. She vacuumed (above) the windows and (under) the bed.

4. (With) a toothbrush, she scrubbed (between) the bathroom tiles.

5. (Despite) Yvette's backbreaking efforts, Augusta complained (about) cat hair.

Exercise 2

1. Augusta was married (to) a psychiatrist.

2. This psychiatrist loved Augusta (despite) her peculiarities.

3. (Before) their wedding, she wept (for) hours.

4. (During) the ceremony, she insisted (on) the presence (of) her African grey parrot, Marmaduke.

5. A bird (with) such a wide and colorful vocabulary can be an embarrassment.

6. It shouted (at) the minister.

7. It cursed (during) the vows.

8. (Throughout) the reception, it nibbled (at) the Waldorf salad.

9. These exotic birds live (for) forty (to) fifty years.

10. (Despite) this whole experience, the psychiatrist settled (into) marriage (with) Augusta.

Exercise 3

1. [Augusta] was married to a psychiatrist.

2. [This psychiatrist] loved Augusta despite her peculiarities.

3. Before their wedding, [she] wept for hours.

4. During the ceremony, [she] insisted on the presence of her African grey parrot, Marmaduke.

5. [A bird with such a wide and colorful vocabulary] can be an embarrassment.

6. [It] shouted at the minister.

7. [It] cursed during the vows.

8. Throughout the reception, [it] nibbled at the Waldorf salad.

9. [These exotic birds] live for forty to fifty years.

10. Despite this whole experience, [the psychiatrist] settled into marriage with Augusta.

Exercise 4

1. [Forcing her way, Belinda] reached the autograph table of Margo Maven.
   MV

2. [Belinda] had been looking forward to this day.
   HV HV   MV

3. [Margo, glancing up at Belinda,] suddenly frowned.
   MV

$$\overset{\text{HV \quad MV}}{}$$

4. [She] <u>was recalling</u> Belinda's face.

5. [Poor <u>Belinda</u>, just doing her job as a police officer,] <u>had ticketed</u> the big star last week.

_{HV   MV}

Exercise 5

1. [Determined to win, <u>Bernardo</u>] <u>practiced</u> the entire weekend.

2. [<u>Bernardo</u>, determined to win], <u>practiced</u> the entire weekend.

3. [An enthusiastic <u>crowd</u>] <u>filled</u> the gym.

4. [The <u>crowd</u>, filled with enthusiasm,] <u>cheered</u> Bernardo.

5. [A <u>crowd</u> filled with enthusiasm] <u>awaited</u> his entrance.

Exercise 6

1. [O'Malley] <u>wanted</u> to visit the ruins of ancient Egypt.

2. To get there, [he] <u>had booked</u> a flight to Cairo.

3. [His <u>plans</u> to visit Luxor] <u>required</u> an overnight train trip.

4. [He] <u>had failed</u> in earlier attempts to visit this cradle of civilization.

5. To assure success this time, [O'Malley] <u>hired</u> a reputable guide to oversee the entire adventure.

Chapter Six

Exercise 1

1. (Wherever) <u>we went</u>, we were suspicious of everybody.

2. (If) <u>others brushed close to us</u>, we feared (that) <u>they might be pickpockets</u>.

3. (After) <u>we had breakfast</u>, we toured the Fine Arts Museum.

4. I felt safe (as long as) <u>we stayed in the galleries</u>.

5. (Since) <u>art lovers are supposed to have solid values</u>, we assumed (that) <u>we had no problem.</u>.

6. (As) we walked into the new wing, we came upon a new exhibit called The Romance of Thievery.

7. (Whether) I was being paranoid or not, I felt threatened among these paintings of rosy-cheeked street urchins and bearded con-artists.

8. I became panicky (whenever) we saw anything connected with purse snatching.

9. (When) we finished the tour, I had developed a nervous twitch.

10. Some people remain nervous (until) they accept the basic insecurity of life.

Exercise 2

1. Wherever we went, [we] were suspicious of everybody.

2. If others brushed close to us, [we] feared that they might be pickpockets.

3. After we had breakfast, [we] toured the Fine Arts Museum.

4. [I] felt safe as long as we stayed in the galleries.

5. Since art lovers are supposed to have solid values, [we] assumed that we had no problem.

6. As we walked into the new wing, [we] came upon a new exhibit called The Romance of Thievery.

7. Whether I was being paranoid or not, [I] felt threatened among these paintings of rosy-cheeked street urchins and bearded con-artists.

8. [I] became panicky whenever we saw anything connected with purse snatching.

9. When we finished the tour, [I] had developed a nervous twitch.

10. [Some people] remain nervous until they accept the basic insecurity of life.

Exercise 3

1. The town (where) my cousins live is filled with generous if eccentric millionaires.

2. Those (who) like big money and unusual people would love the place.

3. Patricia Hernandez, a big-hearted woman (who) loves animals, has contributed over $500,000 to the care of stray cats.

4. These cats (that) she supports have grown to be plump, beautiful, and demanding.

5. Jim Hawkins, (who) made his money on strawberry preserves, supports the town's Museum of Jams and Jellies.

6. The nation's only museum (that) features spreadable sweets, this institution attracts tourists from all parts of the country.

7. Marmalandia, (which) opened last year, is its most popular exhibit.

8. Otis Blinker, a feisty industrialist (who) once arm wrestled Edsel Ford, financed the town's architetural centerpiece, a 10-story bell tower (that) tolls on the hour.

9. A man (who) loves anything that rings, Blinker visits the tower regularly.

10. His favorite bar, (which) is located across the street, allows him to savor many a concert.

Exercise 4

1. [The town where my cousins live] is filled with generous if eccentric millionaires.

2. [Those who like big money and unusual people] would love the place.

3. [Patricia Hernandez, a big-hearted woman who loves animals,] has contributed over $500,000 to the care of stray cats.

4. [These cats that she supports] have grown to be plump, beautiful, and demanding.

5. [Jim Hawkins, who made his money on strawberry preserves,] supports the town's Museum of Jams and Jellies.

6. [The nation's only museum that features spreadable sweets, this institution] attracts tourists from all parts of the country.

7. [Marmalandia, which opened last year,] is its most popular exhibit.

8. [Otis Blinker, a feisty industrialist who once arm-wrestled Edsel Ford,] financed the town's architectural centerpiece, a 10-story bell tower that tolls on the hour.

9. [A man who loves anything that rings, Blinker] visits the tower regularly.

10. [His favorite bar, which is located across the street,] allows him to savor many a concert.

Chapter Seven

Exercise 1

1. Mt. Lassen, (which) is a 10,453 foot volcano (located) fifty miles east (of) Redding, California, last erupted (in) 1917.

2. Mt. Lassen, a volcano (located) fifty miles east (of) Redding, California, last erupted (in) 1917.

3. Lassen belongs (to) the Circle of Fire, (which) is a series (of) volcanoes (that) ring the Pacific Ocean.

4. (About) 11,000 years ago, (while) glaciers still covered this area, a one-cubic mile dome (of) semi-solid lava thrust (from) the earth.

5. (In) 1917, an endless flow (of) steaming lava, (undeterred) (by) the under- lying rock, devastated the mountainside.

6. (Moving) ever forward, the lava toppled great stands (of) old-growth forest.

7. (Over) two hundred miles away, San Franciscans were shocked (to) see the sky darken.

8. Today, Lassen National Park is one (of) the least known (of) the National Parks.

9. (Although) steam was still visible (in) summit craters (until) the early 1940's, only thin wisps appear today.

10. But (in) one part (of) the park, steaming fumeroles give evidence (of) the power (that) remains (under) the ground.

Exercise 2

1. [Mt. Lassen, which is a 10,453 foot volcano located fifty miles east of Redding, California,] last erupted in 1917.

2. [Mt. Lassen, a volcano located fifty miles east of Redding, California,] last erupted in 1917.

3. [Lassen] belongs to the Circle of Fire, which is a series of volcanoes that ring the Pacific Ocean.

4. About 11,000 years ago, while glaciers still covered this area,[a one-cubic mile dome of semi-solid lava] thrust from the earth.

5. In 1917, [an endless flow of steaming lava, undeterred by the overlying rock,] devastated the mountainside.

6. [Moving ever forward, the lava] toppled great stands of old-growth forest.

7. Over two hundred miles away, [San Franciscans] were shocked to see the sky darken.

8. Today, [Lassen Nationa Park] is one of the least known of the National Parks.

9. Although steam was still visible in summit craters until the early 1940's, [only thin wisps] appear today.

10. But in one part of the park, [steaming fumeroles] give evidence of the power that remains under the ground.

Exercise 3

1. [To get rich] was Martha's lifelong goal.

2. To win the lottery, [she] bought $100 worth of tickets each payday.

3. [Whoever wins the lottery] will live well for years to come.

4. [That Martha knew this] was clear to us all.

5. [Winning 10 million dollars] would allow her to jet around the world and to eat whatever she wanted.

6. [Hoping to be the first millionaire in her family, Martha] had speculated in real estate.

7. To get started, [she] purchased a tiny cabin in Virginia.

8. Unfortunately, [repairing a an old log cabin] takes skill and money.

9. At the end of two years, [the cabin] had become home to a family of skunks.

10. [To clear them out] would have cost considerable effort and money.

Exercise 4

1. The newspapers said that [Senator Methuselah] had slept throughout the entire congressional session.

2. It is thought that [Methuselah] is over 100 years old.

3. Senator Ratchet said [the ancient legislator] was acquainted with Theodore Roosevelt.

4. Andrea Bernstein once wrote: "[Senator Methuselah] is our connection with history, our touchstone with the nation's founders."

5. Methuselah believes that [we] should reelect Grover Cleveland.

Exercise 5

1. There <u>were</u> [50,000 <u>people</u>] at the Gloomray concert.

2. There <u>was</u> [a hard-core <u>crowd</u>] at the foot of the stage.

3. There <u>were</u> [a few enthusiastic <u>fans</u>] <u>holding</u> up sequin-covered signs that welcomed Gloomray.

4. There <u>was</u> [deafening <u>applause</u>] when Gloomray strutted onto the stage.

5. There <u>was</u> [a 300-pound security <u>guard</u>] <u>standing</u> at the stage door.